BEGINNING BRIDGE QUIZZES

by Michael Penick

**Published by
Devyn Press, Inc.
Louisville, Kentucky**

Illustrations by Jude Goodwin

Printed in the United States of America.

Devyn Press, Inc.
151 Thierman Lane
Louisville, KY 40207

ISBN 0-910791-67-8

TABLE OF CONTENTS

DEDICATION

For Lauren, Nancy, Gayle, Brenda, Jeanna, Jo, Karen, Dianne and Eileen — Lovely ladies all.

INTRODUCTION

The purpose of *Beginning Bridge Quizzes* is to help you check your knowledge of all aspects of beginning bridge by solving problems. *Beginning Bridge Quizzes* presents questions and problems on all facets of beginning bridge — from counting points through bidding, play and defense.

While this book may be used independent of any other text, the first fourteen chapters in *Beginning Bridge Quizzes* are coordinated with the fourteen chapters contained in my first book, *Beginning Bridge Complete,* and are ideal for use with that text. These practical quizzes are certain to help you improve. Don't be discouraged if you miss some of the questions. Remember, if you never miss a question, you are no longer a beginner! If you do encounter difficulty with any of the quizzes, consult the appropriate chapter of *Beginning Bridge Complete.*

Chapter fifteen consists of a long "final exam" which tests you on all aspects of beginning bridge. This chapter will not only let you grade yourself, but will also show you the areas that need further review. Have fun!

NOTE TO TEACHERS: This book is ideal for use as a workbook for your beginning bridge courses. I recommend that when you assign the student Chapter One of *Beginning Bridge Complete,* you also assign Chapter One of *Beginning Bridge Quizzes.* I begin each class by reviewing these quiz questions, and I have found that the extra practice strongly reinforces the materials covered in the text and in the classroom.

CHAPTER 1

COUNTING POINTS

In order to know what to bid, you must first evaluate your hand. This is achieved by counting points. The charts below summarize high card points, distributional points, and the rank of suits.

High Card Points (HCPs)

Each Ace . . . . .4 points
Each King . . . . .3 points
Each Queen . . . . .2 points
Each Jack. . . . . .1 point

Distributional Points

Each Void . . . . .3 points
Each Singleton* . . . . .2 points
Each Doubleton* . . . . .1 point

---

*Count no distributional point for a doubleton queen or doubleton jack. Hence, a doubleton queen is worth a total of two points and a doubleton jack is worth a total of one point. If you have a singleton king, queen or jack, count only one distributional point for that singleton.

RANKING

Notrump

Spades

Hearts

Diamonds

Clubs

The rank of suits is shown in the chart above, with notrump being the highest ranking and clubs the lowest ranking suit.

BIDDING & PLAY

You may bid 1 through 7 in any suit or notrump. When playing the hand, the first six tricks won by declarer are called the "book," or "making book." There are 13 tricks in every hand of bridge, so the highest bid possible is a bid at the seven level.

QUIZ NO. 1

For each hand below, decide:
- A. How many high card points do you hold?
- B. How many distributional points do you hold?
- C. How many total points does the hand contain?

1. ♠ J 9 3 2   A. _____
    ♡ K 10 5 3   B. _____
    ◇ A Q 2   C. _____
    ♣ 8 6

2. ♠ A K 5 4 2   A. _____
    ♡ 9   B. _____
    ◇ Q J 7   C. _____
    ♣ 10 9 8 6

3. ♠ Q 10 3   A. _____
    ♡ K J 9 8 3 2   B. _____
    ◇ —   C. _____
    ♣ K J 6 2

4. ♠ Q   A. _____
    ♡ Q 9 3 2   B. _____
    ◇ A J 8 5   C. _____
    ♣ A Q 9 8

5. ♠ A 9 8 6 4   A. _____
    ♡ A Q 8 5   B. _____
    ◇ 7 6   C. _____
    ♣ 7 3

6. ♠ A Q 8 7 5 4 3 2   A. _____
    ♡ —   B. _____
    ◇ 6   C. _____
    ♣ Q 8 7 5

9

7. ♠ Q 7 6   A. _____
   ♡ A K 7   B. _____
   ♢ J 9 7 3   C. _____
   ♣ K Q J

8. ♠ K   A. _____
   ♡ 9 8 6 4 2   B. _____
   ♢ 7 6 4 3   C. _____
   ♣ Q J 3

9. ♠ A 5   A. _____
   ♡ J 6 5 3 2   B. _____
   ♢ Q 9 7 5   C. _____
   ♣ 7 5

10. ♠ A 6 5 4   A. _____
    ♡ K 7   B. _____
    ♢ 8   C. _____
    ♣ Q J 7 6 4 2

11. ♠ Q 2   A. _____
    ♡ J 6 5 4 2   B. _____
    ♢ K 5 4 3 2   C. _____
    ♣ A

12. ♠ Q 9 7   A. _____
    ♡ K 8 6 4   B. _____
    ♢ J 6   C. _____
    ♣ A 7 6 3

13. ♠ A K Q   A. _____
    ♡ A K Q   B. _____
    ♢ A K Q   C. _____
    ♣ A K Q J

14. Which suit is higher ranking — Spades or Diamonds?
_____

15. Which suit is lower ranking — Diamonds or Hearts?
_____

16. What is the lowest ranking suit? _____

MULTIPLE CHOICE:
17. Notrump outranks — (a) Spades; (b) Hearts; (c) Diamonds; (d) Clubs; (e) All of the above; or (f) None of the above.
_____

THE FIRST STEP TOWARD ACCURATE BIDDING IS TO COUNT YOUR POINTS CAREFULLY.

ANSWERS TO QUIZ NO. 1

1. A. 10   B. 1   C. 11

2. A. 10   B. 2   C. 12

3. A. 10   B. 3   C. 13

4. A. 15   B. 1   C. 16

5. A. 10   B. 2   C. 12

6. A. 8   B. 5   C. 13

7. A. 16   B. 0   C. 16

8. A. 6   B. 1   C. 7

9. A. 7   B. 2   C. 9

10. A. 10   B. 3   C. 13

11. A. 10   B. 2   C. 12

12. A. 10   B. 0   C. 10

13. A. 37   B. 0   C. 37

14. Spades

15. Diamonds

16. Clubs

17. (e)

CHAPTER 2

SCORING

Contracts bid and made	Points
Clubs	20 points for each trick, scored below the line
Diamonds	20 points for each trick, scored below the line
Hearts	30 points for each trick, scored below the line
Spades	30 points for each trick, scored below the line
Notrump	40 points for the first trick, and 30 points for each succeeding trick, scored below the line

Overtricks

Clubs & Diamonds	20 points for each extra trick, scored above the line
Hearts, Spades & Notrump	30 points for each extra trick, scored above the line

Score required for game . . . . 100 points

Bonuses for rubbers

if first two games won . . . . 700 points
if two out of three games won . . . . 500 points

Slam Bonuses

Small slam, not vulnerable . . . . 500 points
Small slam, vulnerable . . . . 750 points
Grand slam, not vulnerable . . . . 1000 points
Grand slam, vulnerable . . . . 1500 points

Honors

The honor cards in a suit contract are the AKQJ10 of
    trumps.
The honor cards at notrump are the four aces.

100 for four trump honors in one hand
150 for all five trump honors in one hand
150 for all four aces in one hand at notrump.
(May be won by declarer or defender.)

Bonuses for making doubled contracts:

A. Double your bid score below the line
B. 50 point bonus plus 100 points for each overtrick if
    not vulnerable and 200 points for each overtrick if
    vulnerable, scored above the line

Bonuses for making redoubled contracts:

A. Quadruple your bid score below the line
B. 50 point bonus plus twice the doubled score for each
    overtrick scored above the line.

Penalties

What you score if you set the opponents' contract:

50 per trick, undoubled, not vulnerable
100 per trick, undoubled, vulnerable
100 for first trick, plus
   200 for every trick thereafter, doubled, not vulnerable
200 for first trick, plus
   300 for every trick thereafter, doubled, vulnerable

If redoubled, multiply the doubled penalty by two.

QUIZ NO. 2

You sit down with your favorite partner for a rubber of bridge. It takes eleven hands to complete the rubber. The result of each hand is shown below.

Assuming you and your partner are "WE," and your opponents are "THEY,", place your results appropriately on the chart on the next page.

1. You and your partner bid and make 2 ♠
2. You and your partner bid 1 ♢ and make 9 tricks
3. You and your partner bid 1 ♡ and go down 1 trick
4. You and your partner bid 2 ♢ and make 8 tricks
5. Your opponents bid 3 ♡, you double and the opponents go down 2 tricks
6. You and your partner bid 4 ♠ and go down 2 tricks
7. You and your partner bid 3 NT, are doubled, and go down 2 tricks
8. Your opponents bid 3 NT and go down 3 tricks
9. Your opponents bid 1 ♡, you double, and the opponents make 8 tricks
10. Your opponents bid 2 ♢, you double, and the opponents make 8 tricks
11. You and your partner bid 6 ♡ and make 12 tricks
12. The rubber is concluded. Compute the total score for each side.

WE   *THEY*

ANSWERS TO QUIZ NO. 2

The numbers in parentheses correspond to the numbers of the questions on page 16.

	WE			THEY	
				50	(10)
(11)	750			100	(9)
(11)	500			50	(9)
(8)	150			500	(7)
(5)	300			200	(6)
(2)	40			50	(3)
(1)	60				
(2)	20				
(4)	40				
				60	(9)
				80	(10)
(11)	180				

(12) TOTAL POINTS: WE   2,040   points

                        THEY   1,090   points

CHAPTER 3

OPENING BID OF ONE OF A SUIT

PROCEDURE TO DETERMINE WHAT TO OPEN

Step 1: Arrange your cards into suits.

Step 2: Count your high card points and your distributional points.

With fewer than 13 points, pass.
With 13 to 21 points, open the bidding.

(a) Look for your longest suit. If it is a five-card or longer major suit, open the bidding with one of that major suit (with five spades and five hearts, open 1 ♠).

(b) If the longest suit in the hand is not a major suit of five or more cards, open the minor suit with the most cards in it.

(c) If the longest suit in the hand is not a major suit of five or more cards and the minor suits are of equal length, open 1 ♢ with 4-4, 5-5, or 6-6 in the minor suits, but open 1 ♣ with 3-3 in the minor suits.

With more than 21 points, open with a bid at the two level or higher.

QUIZ NO. 3

For each of the following, decide:
   A. How many points do you have (including distribution)?
   B. What is your opening bid?

1. ♠ 7 5 4 3   A. _____
    ♡ K 4 3   B. _____
    ◇ A 8 5
    ♣ J 5 4

2. ♠ 5 4   A. _____
    ♡ 6 5 3   B. _____
    ◇ A K J 7 2
    ♣ K Q 3

3. ♠ 7 6 3   A. _____
    ♡ K Q J 5 4   B. _____
    ◇ A J 9 5
    ♣ 5

4. ♠ Q J 9 8 6   A. _____
    ♡ A K Q 6 5   B. _____
    ◇ 8
    ♣ 5 3

5. ♠ A J 4   A. _____
    ♡ 8 6   B. _____
    ◇ Q 9 8 4
    ♣ A K 8 2

6. ♠ 6 5 3   A. _____
    ♡ A J 9 3   B. _____
    ◇ Q 9 8
    ♣ A K 8

7. ♠ A 3   A. _____
   ♥ 9 8   B. _____
   ♦ 9 8 6 4 3
   ♣ A K J 7

8. ♠ 9 8 6 4 2   A. _____
   ♥ 8   B. _____
   ♦ A K Q 7 3
   ♣ K 8

9. ♠ 5   A. _____
   ♥ —   B. _____
   ♦ Q J 9 8 6 4
   ♣ A K Q 6 5 3

10. ♠ A K 7 5 3   A. _____
    ♥ A K 9 8 5 2   B. _____
    ♦ 6
    ♣ 8

11. ♠ K J 5 4   A. _____
    ♥ K Q 9 2   B. _____
    ♦ A 7
    ♣ 9 8 5

12. ♠ A 9 5   A. _____
    ♥ K 7 3   B. _____
    ♦ 9 8 6 4
    ♣ A Q J

13. ♠ A 2   A. _____
    ♥ A K Q   B. _____
    ♦ 9 8 7 5
    ♣ A Q 8 5

14. ♠ Q 2
♡ A K Q 5 3
◇ A 8 6 4
♣ J 7

A. _____
B. _____

15. ♠ Q J 6
♡ K 5 3 2
◇ A K 7
♣ 9 7 6

A. _____
B. _____

OPENING BIDS OF ONE OF A SUIT

ANSWERS TO QUIZ NO. 3

1. A. 8   B. Pass

2. A. 14   B. 1 ♦

3. A. 13   B. 1 ♡

4. A. 15   B. 1 ♠

5. A. 15   B. 1 ♦

6. A. 14   B. 1 ♣

7. A. 14   B. 1 ♦

8. A. 15   B. 1 ♠

9. A. 17   B. 1 ♦

10. A. 18   B. 1 ♡

11. A. 14   B. 1 ♣

12. A. 14   B. 1 ♦

13. A. 20   B. 1 ♦

14. A. 16   B. 1 ♡

15. A. 13   B. 1 ♣

CHAPTER 4

STRONG TWOS AND PREEMPTS

The opening bid of two of a suit tells partner that you have a very strong hand. You should have close to sufficient strength to make game by yourself to open with a strong two bid.

An opening bid of three of a suit shows a weak hand. Its purpose is to make life difficult for the opponents by disrupting their lines of communication. This is a preemptive bid.

Requirements to open the bidding with two of a suit (strong two bid)

1. 22 or more points
2. A suit of five or more cards

Requirements to open the bidding with three of a suit (preemptive bid)

1. A suit at least seven cards in length
2. Three to nine high card points

QUIZ NO. 4

For each of the following, answer:
  A. How many points do you have (including distribution)?
  B. What is your opening bid?

1. ♠ A K Q 5 4   A. _____
   ♡ A K 4 3   B. _____
   ◊ A 4
   ♣ Q 6

2. ♠ 4   A. _____
   ♡ 3 2   B. _____
   ◊ K Q J 8 6 5 4
   ♣ 8 7 5

3. ♠ 8 7   A. _____
   ♡ 7   B. _____
   ◊ 8 7 5
   ♣ J 9 8 7 6 5 3

4. ♠ A   A. _____
   ♡ A K Q 8 6 2   B. _____
   ◊ A K 8 6
   ♣ J 4

5. ♠ 8   A. _____
   ♡ A K Q 9 7 4   B. _____
   ◊ Q 9 7 5
   ♣ A 8

6. ♠ A K 9 8 7 5 3   A. _____
   ♡ 8   B. _____
   ◊ 8 7 5
   ♣ 8 6

7. ♠ 7 6
   ♡ 7
   ◇ 8 6 3
   ♣ Q J 9 8 6 5 3

   A. _____
   B. _____

8. ♠ A K 9 8 6
   ♡ A K 9 8 6
   ◇ A 2
   ♣ A

   A. _____
   B. _____

9. ♠ K 8
   ♡ 9
   ◇ A Q J 8 7
   ♣ A K Q J 8

   A. _____
   B. _____

10. ♠ 9 8
    ♡ A Q J 9 8 6 5
    ◇ 8 7
    ♣ 7 6

    A. _____
    B. _____

A STRONG TWO BID CAN BE VERY
INTIMIDATING TO YOUR OPPONENTS.

ANSWERS TO QUIZ NO. 4

1. A. 23   B.   2♠

2. A. 9   B.   3♦

3. A. 4   B.   Pass

4. A. 23   B.   2♥

5. A. 18   B.   1♥

6. A. 10   B.   3♠

7. A. 6   B.   3♣

8. A. 25   B.   2♠

9. A. 23   B.   2♦

10. A. 10   B.   3♥

CHAPTER 5

NOTRUMP BIDDING

Requirements for opening with a notrump bid

1. To open with 1 notrump, 2 notrump, or 3 notrump, you must have a notrump type hand. To qualify as a notrump hand, the distribution of your cards must be one of the following:

   a. 4-3-3-3
   b. 4-4-3-2
   c. 5-3-3-2

   A notrump hand has no voids or singletons, and not more than one doubleton.

2. Assuming you have a notrump hand, you must next determine whether you have the appropriate number of high card points to open the bidding with a notrump bid. Those requirements are as follows:

   a. 1 notrump - 16 to 18 high card points
   b. 2 notrump - 22 to 24 high card points
   c. 3 notrump - 25 to 27 high card points

   If your hand meets these requirements open 1, 2 or 3 notrump, as appropriate.

Procedure to determine the proper opening bid on any hand.

Step 1: Arrange your cards into suits.

Step 2: Determine whether your hand is of the notrump type.

Step 3: Count your high card points and your distributional points. If you have enough points to open the bidding and a notrump-type hand, then check to see whether your number of high card points fits the requirements for opening bids of 1, 2 or 3 Notrump. If so, open the bidding the appropriate number of notrump. If not, follow the steps outlined for opening suit bids set out in the chart on page 19.

QUIZ NO. 5

For each of the following hands, indicate your proper opening bid:

1. ♠ K 7 5
   ♡ A 9 8
   ◊ Q 4 3 2
   ♣ A K 6

   Opening Bid _____

2. ♠ A K
   ♡ A Q J 6
   ◊ A K 8 2
   ♣ A J 5

   Opening Bid _____

3. ♠ K J 8 6
   ♡ A K 8 6
   ◊ A 7
   ♣ A K J

   Opening Bid _____

4. ♠ J 9 7 6 5
   ♡ A Q
   ◊ K J 7
   ♣ A Q 3

   Opening Bid _____

5. ♠ 8 7 5
   ♡ K 6
   ◊ A K Q 9 4
   ♣ K J 7

   Opening Bid _____

6. ♠ J 8 7 6 4
   ♡ A Q
   ◊ A K Q 8
   ♣ 8 7

   Opening Bid _____

7. ♠ K Q 8 6
   ♡ A Q J
   ◊ K Q J
   ♣ A J 5

   Opening Bid _____

8. ♠ A 8 7
   ♡ K 6 5 4
   ◊ A 3 2
   ♣ Q 4 3

   Opening Bid _____

9. ♠ Q 7
   ♡ J 8
   ◊ A K 9 8
   ♣ A Q 8 7 5

   Opening Bid _____

10. ♠ 3 2
    ♡ A K Q 4
    ◊ K 8 6
    ♣ A J 5 4

    Opening Bid _____

11. ♠ A Q 9 8 7
    ♡ K 7
    ◇ A 3 2
    ♣ Q 5 4

    Opening Bid _____

12. ♠ A Q J 9 7
    ♡ K 6
    ◇ A 7 4
    ♣ Q 6 3

    Opening Bid _____

13. ♠ A Q J 9 7 3
    ♡ K 8
    ◇ K 8 4
    ♣ K J

    Opening Bid _____

14. ♠ K Q 3
    ♡ A Q 9 6 4
    ◇ A K
    ♣ A J 7

    Opening Bid _____

15. ♠ A 8 6
    ♡ K 7 6
    ◇ Q 4 3 2
    ♣ J 7 2

    Opening Bid _____

16. ♠ A K J
    ♡ A K Q 7
    ◇ K 9 8
    ♣ A Q 2

    Opening Bid _____

17. ♠ K Q 5
    ♡ A Q 8 7 5
    ◇ A
    ♣ A K J 8

    Opening Bid _____

18. ♠ A K 9 8 7 6 3
    ♡ A 4
    ◇ 9 3
    ♣ 7 4

    Opening Bid _____

19. ♠ A K 8 7 5 4 3
    ♡ 8 4
    ◇ 9 3
    ♣ 8 4

    Opening Bid _____

20. ♠ K J 8
    ♡ A 9 5
    ◇ Q 4 3
    ♣ A Q 9 5

    Opening Bid _____

LEARN CORRECT
NOTRUMP BIDDING TO
LAY A SOLID
FOUNDATION FOR
YOUR BRIDGE
UNDERSTANDING.

ANSWERS TO QUIZ NO. 5

1. 1 Notrump
2. 3 Notrump
3. 2 Notrump
4. 1 Notrump
5. 1 Notrump
6. 1 ♠
7. 2 Notrump
8. 1 ♣
9. 1 ♣
10. 1 Notrump

11. 1 ♠
12. 1 Notrump
13. 1 ♠
14. 2 Notrump
15. Pass
16. 3 Notrump
17. 2 ♡
18. 1 ♠
19. 3 ♠
20. 1 Notrump

CHAPTER 6

GAMES AND SLAMS

Bonus points are awarded for bidding and making games and slams. The game bid in Notrump is 3 Notrump, which requires the taking of nine tricks. A game bid in Hearts or Spades is 4♡/4♠, which requires the taking of ten tricks. A game bid in Clubs or Diamonds is 5♣/5♢, which requires that eleven tricks be taken.

The partnership may contract for a small slam by bidding at the six level (12 tricks), or a grand slam by bidding at the seven level (13 tricks).

The charts below set out the combined assets which you and your partner should hold if the partnership is to have a reasonable expectation of making a game or slam.

Point Requirements to Bid Games and Slams	
Game Contract	Points Required to Have A Reasonable Expectation To Make
1. 3 Notrump	26 points (high card points only)
2. 4♡	26 points
3. 4♠	26 points
4. 5♣	29 points
5. 5♢	29 points

Slams	Points Required to Have A Reasonable Expectation To Make
1. Small slam	33 points
2. Grand slam	37 points

QUIZ NO. 6

For each of the following, state:
- A. What are the combined assets (total points) of the North and South hands (including distribution)?
- B. What should the final contract be?

	North	*South*			
1.	♠ A J 6 4 2	♠ K 8 7 3	(A)	North	_____
	♡ 8	♡ A 9 7 5		South	_____
	◊ A K 5	◊ 8 7 4		Total	_____
	♣ Q 8 6 4	♣ K 5	(B)	_____	
2.	♠ Q 9 5	♠ K 8 7 4	(A)	North	_____
	♡ A 9 6 3	♡ K 7 5		South	_____
	◊ K Q 7	◊ A J 9 5		Total	_____
	♣ A J 5	♣ Q 2	(B)	_____	
3.	♠ 5 3	♠ 4 2	(A)	North	_____
	♡ A 7 6 4	♡ 5		South	_____
	◊ K Q 9 8 6	◊ A J 10 7 5 3		Total	_____
	♣ K 6	♣ A Q J 5	(B)	_____	
4.	♠ Q 10 4 2	♠ K 6 3	(A)	North	_____
	♡ K 5	♡ A 6		South	_____
	◊ A Q 7 5 2	◊ K 8 6 3		Total	_____
	♣ 8 5	♣ A Q 10 4	(B)	_____	
5.	♠ 6	♠ A J 5	(A)	North	_____
	♡ A K J 6 4	♡ Q 8 7		South	_____
	◊ 6 5 3	◊ K Q J 10		Total	_____
	♣ K J 8 6	♣ A Q 5	(B)	_____	
6.	♠ A K Q	♠ 6 5 4	(A)	North	_____
	♡ A J 6 5	♡ K Q 9		South	_____
	◊ K Q 8	◊ A J 7 6		Total	_____
	♣ A K 2	♣ J 7 4	(B)	_____	

7.   ♠ A Q 9   ♠ K J 8   (A)   North ____
      ♡ K 8 7 5   ♡ A Q 9 6   South ____
      ◊ 9 8 6 4   ◊ 7   Total ____
      ♣ J 7   ♣ K Q 9 8 5   (B) _____

8.   ♠ A Q 3   ♠ K J 8   (A)   North ____
      ♡ 8 7   ♡ A J 9 5   South ____
      ◊ J 7 6 2   ◊ 4   Total ____
      ♣ A J 9 5   ♣ K Q 8 6 4   (B) _____

9.   ♠ A Q 9 8   ♠ K J 7 6 5   (A)   North ____
      ♡ 8   ♡ A J 7   South ____
      ◊ K J 4 3   ◊ Q 5 2   Total ____
      ♣ K Q 5 4   ♣ 8 6   (B) _____

10. ♠ K 7 5   ♠ Q J 9   (A)   North ____
      ♡ A 6 4   ♡ K Q 5 3   South ____
      ◊ K Q 9 8 5   ◊ A J 7   Total ____
      ♣ Q 4   ♣ A K 3   (B) _____

*LEARN THE REQUIREMENTS FOR OPENING BIDS,
GAMES AND SLAMS.*

39

ANSWERS TO QUIZ NO. 6

1. (A) North — 16
        South — 11
        Total — 27
    (B) 4 ♠

2. (A) North — 16
        South — 13
        Total — 29
    (B) 3 Notrump

3. (A) North — 14
        South — 15
        Total — 29
    (B) 5 ♦

4. (A) North — 13 (11 HCPs)
        South — 17 (16 HCPs)
        Total — 30 (27 HCPs)
    (B) 3 Notrump

5. (A) North — 14
        South — 19
        Total — 33
    (B) 6 ♥

6. (A) North — 26
        South — 11
        Total — 37
    (B) 7 Notrump

7. (A) North — 10
        South — 17
        Total — 27
    (B) 4 ♥

8. (A) North — 13
        South — 16
        Total — 29
    (B) 5 ♣

9. (A) North — 17
        South — 12
        Total — 29
    (B) 4 ♠

10. (A) North — 14
        South — 20
        Total — 34
    (B) 6 Notrump

Responses to Opening Bids of 1 ♡ or 1 ♠

A. With 0 to 5 points, pass.

B. With 6 to 9 points:
1. With 3 or more cards in partner's major suit, raise partner's major suit to the two level.
2. Bid a four-card or longer major suit at the one level.
3. If you cannot proceed under Step 1 or 2 above, bid 1 Notrump.

C. With 10 to 12 points:
1. Bid a major suit of four or more cards at the one level.
2. Bid a new suit at the two level.

D. With 13 to 15 points:
1. With four or more cards in partner's suit, raise partner's suit to the three level.
2. Bid your longest suit at the lowest level possible. With two suits of equal length, bid the major. With two minors of equal length, bid 2 ♢.
3. With a balanced hand, bid 2 NT.

E. With 16 to 18 points:
1. Bid your longest suit at the lowest level possible. With two suits of equal length, bid a major in preference to a minor; if both suits are minors, bid 2 ♢.
2. With a notrump-type hand and no four-card or longer major, bid 3 Notrump.

F. Jump shift with 19 or more points.

Responses to Opening Bids of 1♣ or 1♦

A. With 0 to 5 points, pass.

B. With 6 to 9 points:

1. Bid your longest suit at the one level. With two four-card suits, bid the lower-ranking; with two five- or six-card suits, bid the higher-ranking.
2. With four or more cards in partner's minor suit, raise partner's minor suit to the two level.
3. If you cannot proceed under Step 1 or 2 above, bid 1 Notrump.

C. With 10 to 12 points:

1. Bid your longest suit at the one level.
2. If you cannot bid a suit at the one level, bid your longest suit at the two level.

D. With 13 to 15 points:

1. Bid your longest suit at the lowest level possible.
2. Bid 2 Notrump with a notrump-type hand.

E. With 16 to 18 points:

1. Bid your longest suit at the lowest level possible.
2. Bid 3 Notrump with a notrump-type hand.

F. Jump shift with 19 or more points.

Responses to Opening Bids of 2♣, 2◊, 2♡ and 2♠

A. With 0 to 5 points, bid 2 Notrump as a negative response.

B. With 6 to 8 points, raise partner's suit to the three level with three or more cards in his suit. If you do not have at least three cards in partner's suit, bid any suit of your own containing five or more cards. With fewer than three cards in partner's suit and no suit of five or more cards of your own, bid 3 Notrump.

C. With 9 or more points, consider bidding a slam.

Responses to Opening Bids of 3♣, 3◊, 3♡ and 3♠

A. With 0 to 16 points, pass.

B. With 17 or more points, raise partner's major to game or bid 3 Notrump.

C. With 17 or more points, if partner has preempted a minor suit, bid 3 Notrump or raise partner's minor suit to game.

Determine the correct response on each of the following hands.

1. ♠ 7 6 3
    ♡ K 6 5
    ◇ 5 4
    ♣ Q J 7 5 4

    A. Partner's opening bid: 1 ♠
        Your response: _____
    B. Partner's opening bid: 1 ◇
        Your response: _____

2. ♠ K Q 7 3
    ♡ 6 5
    ◇ 7 2
    ♣ A 9 7 5 3

    A. Partner's opening bid: 1 ◇
        Your response: _____
    B. Partner's opening bid: 1 ♡
        Your response: _____

3. ♠ K 5 2
    ♡ 6 3
    ◇ A 8 6 3
    ♣ A Q 4 3

    A. Partner's opening bid: 1 ♡
        Your response: _____
    B. Partner's opening bid: 1 ◇
        Your response: _____

4. ♠ K 8 7 4
    ♡ K 4
    ◇ 5 4 3
    ♣ A K 6 5

    A. Partner's opening bid: 1 ♡
        Your response: _____
    B. Partner's opening bid: 1 ♠
        Your response: _____

5. ♠ Q 4
    ♡ K 9 7 2
    ◇ 5 4 2
    ♣ K 9 8 6

    A. Partner's opening bid: 1 ♣
        Your response: _____
    B. Partner's opening bid: 1 ♠
        Your response: _____

6. ♠ 6 4
    ♡ A K 9 8 7 5
    ◇ A K 8
    ♣ A J

    A. Partner's opening bid: 1 ♠
        Your response: _____
    B. Partner's opening bid: 1 ◇
        Your response: _____

7. ♠ Q 7   A. Partner's opening bid: 1 ◇
   ♡ K 8 7 6   Your response: _____
   ◇ A J 6   B. Partner's opening bid: 1 ♠
   ♣ K J 7 5   Your response: _____

8. ♠ 6 5   A. Partner's opening bid: 1 ♣
   ♡ Q 4 3   Your response: _____
   ◇ K 7 4   B. Partner's opening bid: 1 ♠
   ♣ Q 6 5 3 2   Your response: _____

9. ♠ J 6 4   A. Partner's opening bid: 1 ◇
   ♡ Q 3 2   Your response: _____
   ◇ 5 4 3   B. Partner's opening bid: 2 ◇
   ♣ 6 5 3 2   Your response: _____

10. ♠ J 6 4   A. Partner's opening bid: 2 ♠
    ♡ K 6   Your response: _____
    ◇ 6 5 4 2   B. Partner's opening bid: 1 ♡
    ♣ Q J 6 4   Your response: _____

11. ♠ 9 7   A. Partner's opening bid: 1 ♣
    ♡ 9 6 4   Your response: _____
    ◇ A K 9 7 5   B. Partner's opening bid: 3 ♣
    ♣ Q 9 8   Your response: _____

12. ♠ K 6   A. Partner's opening bid: 1 ◇
    ♡ A Q 9 2   Your response: _____
    ◇ K J 7   B. Partner's opening bid: 1 ♠
    ♣ K J 8 5   Your response: _____

ALWAYS MAKE THE CORRECT RESPONSE.

1. A. 2♠   B. 1 Notrump

2. A. 1♣   B. 1♠

3. A. 2 Notrump   B. 2 Notrump

4. A. 1♠   B. 3♠

5. A. 1♡   B. 1 Notrump

6. A. 3♡   B. 2♡

7. A. 1♡   B. 2 Notrump

8. A. 2♣   B. 1 Notrump

9. A. Pass   B. 2 Notrump

10. A. 3♠   B. 1 Notrump

11. A. 1♢   B. Pass

12. A. 1♡   B. 3 Notrump

CHAPTER 8

RESPONSES TO OPENING NOTRUMP BIDS

Responses to an Opening Bid of 1 Notrump:

A. With 0 to 7 points:

    1.   With five or more cards in Diamonds, Hearts, or Spades, bid two of that suit.

    2.   With any other hand containing 0 to 7 points, pass.

B. With 8 or 9 points:

    1.   With one or two four-card major suits, bid 2 ♣ (Stayman).

    2.   Without a four-card major, bid 2 Notrump (invitational to game).

C. With 10 to 14 points:

    1.   With one or two four-card major suits, bid 2 ♣ (Stayman).

    2.   With a five-card major suit, bid 3 of that major.

    3.   With a six-card major suit, bid 4 of that major.

    4.   Bid 3 Notrump.

D. With 15 or more points:

    1.   Consider bidding a slam in notrump or your best suit.

Responses to an Opening Bid of 2 Notrump:

A. With 0 to 2 points, pass.

B. With 3 to 10 points, bid as follows:

   1. With five or more cards in Diamonds, Hearts or Spades, bid 3 of that suit.
   2. With one or two four-card major suits, bid 3 ♣ (Stayman).
   3. Bid 3 Notrump.

Responding to an Opening Bid of 3 Notrump:

A. With 0 to 7 points, pass, or bid 4 of a five-card or longer major.

B. With 8 or more points, bid slam in your best suit or in notrump.

Responses to Stayman

A. If you open with a Notrump bid and partner answers by bidding 2 ♣ (Stayman), respond to Stayman as follows:

   1. Holding one four-card major, bid it (2 ♡ or 2 ♠).
   2. Holding two four-card major suits, bid 2 ♠ .
   3. With no four-card major suit, bid 2 ◇ .

B. Over a 2 Notrump opening/3 ♣ (Stayman) or a 3 Notrump opening/4 ♣ (Stayman), the same responses are used at the 3 level or 4 level.

On each of the following hands, partner opens the bidding with either 1 Notrump, 2 Notrump or 3 Notrump. Decide the correct response.

1. You hold:
   ♠ K 8 7 5
   ♡ 7
   ◇ A 8 6 3
   ♣ K 8 6 5

Partner	You
1 Notrump	?

2. You hold:
   ♠ K 9 7 6
   ♡ K 9 8 7
   ◇ 8 6
   ♣ Q 3 2

Partner	You
1 Notrump	?

3. You hold:
   ♠ K 8 6 3
   ♡ K 8 7 6
   ◇ 8 5
   ♣ 8 5 3

Partner	You
1 Notrump	?

4. You hold:
   ♠ K 9 8 7 5 4
   ♡ 7 3
   ◇ 7
   ♣ 7 6 5 3

Partner	You
1 Notrump	?

5. You hold:
   ♠ K 9 8 7 5
   ♡ 7 3 2
   ◇ 7
   ♣ 7 6 5 3

Partner	You
2 Notrump	?

6. You hold:
   ♠ Q 5 3
   ♡ K 8 5
   ◇ 8 5 3
   ♣ A J 8 6

Partner	You
1 Notrump	?

7. You hold:
♠ K 4 3
♥ J 5 4
♦ 8 7 5 3
♣ 7 4 2

Partner
2 Notrump

You
?

8. You hold:
♠ K J 9 8 7
♥ A 9 8
♦ Q 7 5
♣ 8 7

Partner
1 Notrump

You
?

9. You hold:
♠ 8 7 6
♥ K J 8 5
♦ 8 4
♣ 9 7 6 4

Partner
2 Notrump

You
?

10. You hold:
♠ 8 7
♥ K Q 9 8 7 5
♦ A 9
♣ J 9 8

Partner
1 Notrump

You
?

11. You hold:
♠ Q 8 7
♥ J 9 6
♦ K 7 6 5
♣ K 7 5

Partner
3 Notrump

You
?

12. You hold:
♠ 9 4
♥ 8 4
♦ K 8 7 5 3
♣ J 9 8 5

Partner
1 Notrump

You
?

13. You hold:
♠ 7 5
♥ 8 2
♦ J 8 7 4
♣ K 9 8 5 3

Partner
1 Notrump

You
?

14. You hold: ♠ Q 10 9 8 6   *Partner*   *You*
                ♥ 5 4   1 Notrump   ?
                ♦ 8 7
                ♣ 8 7 4 3

15. You hold: ♠ Q 10 8 7   *Partner*   *You*
                ♥ 7 6   1 Notrump   ?
                ♦ K 7
                ♣ K 8 7 5 4

16. You hold: ♠ Q J 5   *Partner*   *You*
                ♥ J 4 3   2 Notrump   ?
                ♦ 8 7 6 4
                ♣ 8 7 5

17. You hold: ♠ Q J 5   *Partner*   *You*
                ♥ J 4 3   1 Notrump   ?
                ♦ 8 7 6 4
                ♣ 8 7 5

18. You hold: ♠ A K 8   *Partner*   *You*
                ♥ K Q 5   1 Notrump   ?
                ♦ A 9 7 4
                ♣ Q 5 4

19. You hold: ♠ 7 4   *Partner*   *You*
                ♥ K 9 7 5 3   1 Notrump   ?
                ♦ 8 7 5 2
                ♣ 3 2

20. You hold: ♠ Q J 10 8 4   *Partner*   *You*
                ♥ 3 2   1 Notrump   ?
                ♦ A 4 3 2
                ♣ K 4

RESPONDING TO 1 NOTRUMP

ANSWERS TO QUIZ NO. 8

1. 2♣

2. 2♣

3. Pass

4. 2♠

5. 3♠

6. 3 Notrump

7. 3 Notrump

8. 3♠

9. 3♣

10. 4♡

11. 6 Notrump

12. 2♢

13. Pass

14. 2♠

15. 2♣

16. 3 Notrump

17. Pass

18. 6 Notrump

19. 2♡

20. 3♠

CHAPTER 9

OPENER'S REBIDS

You open, partner responds, and it is now your second turn to bid. Your second bid is called *opener's rebid*.

As you know, the purpose of the bidding dialogue is to enable you to describe your hand to partner as clearly as possible, utilizing the minimum number of bids necessary to do so. Often, you will be able to give partner a very clear picture of your hand in one or two bids. The following charts demonstrate how this is done:

Opener's Rebid with an Unbalanced (non-notrump) hand

13 to 15 points . . . . Raise responder's suit with four-card support; without support, rebid a six-card or longer suit, or bid a new four-card or longer suit

16 to 18 points . . . . Jump raise partner's suit with four-card support; without support, jump rebid a suit of your own with six or more cards, or bid a new four-card or longer suit

19 to 21 points . . . . Raise partner's suit to the four level with four-card support; jump shift in a suit without support

22 or more points . . . . Open the bidding with two of your longest suit and make the appropriate rebid

---

How opener shows a balanced (notrump) hand

13 to 15 points	Open one of a suit and rebid cheapest notrump
16 to 18 points	Open 1 Notrump
19 to 21 points	Open one of a suit and jump rebid in notrump
22 to 24 points	Open 2 Notrump
25 to 27 points	Open 3 Notrump

For each of the following determine what the proper opening bid should be. The response is given to you. Next, determine opener's rebid.

1. ♠ 6 5
    ♥ A Q J 9 6
    ♦ 9 8 5
    ♣ K Q J

    Opener: _____
    Responder: 1 ♠
    Opener's rebid: _____

2. ♠ 8 7
    ♥ Q J 9 3
    ♦ K Q 6
    ♣ A J 7 4

    Opener: _____
    Responder: 1 ♥
    Opener's rebid: _____

3. ♠ 8 7
    ♥ Q J 9 3
    ♦ K Q 6
    ♣ A J 7 4

    Opener: _____
    Responder: 1 ♠
    Opener's rebid: _____

4. ♠ 6
    ♥ K Q J 9
    ♦ K 9 7 4
    ♣ A K 9 6

    Opener: _____
    Responder: 1 ♥
    Opener's rebid: _____

5. ♠ 8 5
    ♥ A Q 8
    ♦ A Q J 9
    ♣ A Q J 7

    Opener: _____
    Responder: 1 ♠
    Opener's rebid: _____

6. ♠ A Q J 9 8 7
    ♥ A 5
    ♦ 8 7 4
    ♣ A Q

    Opener: _____
    Responder: 1 NT
    Opener's rebid: _____

7. ♠ A Q J 8 7 6   Opener: _____
   ♡ A 5   Responder: 2♣
   ◊ 8 7 4   Opener's rebid: _____
   ♣ A Q

8. ♠ 8 6   Opener: _____
   ♡ A Q J 9 8 5   Responder: 1♠
   ◊ 8 3   Opener's rebid: _____
   ♣ A J 8

9. ♠ 8 6   Opener: _____
   ♡ A Q J 9 8 5   Responder: 2♡
   ◊ 8 3   Opener's rebid: _____
   ♣ A J 8

10. ♠ A Q J 9 5   Opener: _____
    ♡ 7   Responder: 1 NT
    ◊ A 6   Opener's rebid: _____
    ♣ A Q 10 8 3

11. ♠ A Q 8   Opener: _____
    ♡ K Q J 5   Responder: 2♣
    ◊ A Q J 2   Opener's rebid: _____
    ♣ 8 4

12. ♠ A Q 8   Opener: _____
    ♡ K Q J 5   Responder: 1 NT
    ◊ A Q J 2   Opener's rebid: _____
    ♣ 8 4

13. ♠ 6 5 2   Opener: _____
    ♡ A Q J 4   Responder: 1♡
    ◊ A Q   Opener's rebid: _____
    ♣ A K 7 3

14. ♠ 6 5 2
    ♡ A Q J
    ◊ A Q 4
    ♣ A K 7 3

Opener: _____
Responder: 1 ◊
Opener's rebid: _____

15. ♠ 8 4
    ♡ 5
    ◊ A K 9 7
    ♣ A Q J 9 7 3

Opener: _____
Responder: 1 ◊
Opener's rebid: _____

16. ♠ 8 4
    ♡ 5
    ◊ A K 9 7
    ♣ A Q J 9 7 3

Opener: _____
Responder: 1 ♠
Opener's rebid: _____

ANSWERS TO QUIZ NO. 9

1. Opener: 1 ♡
   Opener's rebid: 1 Notrump
2. Opener: 1 ♣
   Opener's rebid: 2 ♡
3. Opener: 1 ♣
   Opener's rebid: 1 Notrump
4. Opener: 1 ◇
   Opener's rebid: 3 ♡
5. Opener: 1 ◇
   Opener's rebid: 2 Notrump
6. Opener: 1 ♠
   Opener's rebid: 3 ♠
7. Opener: 1 ♠
   Opener's rebid: 3 ♠
8. Opener: 1 ♡
   Opener's rebid: 2 ♡
9. Opener: 1 ♡
   Opener's rebid: Pass
10. Opener: 1 ♠
    Opener's rebid: 3 ♣
11. Opener: 1 ◇
    Opener's rebid: 3 Notrump
12. Opener: 1 ◇
    Opener's rebid: 3 Notrump
13. Opener: 1 ♣
    Opener's rebid: 4 ♡
14. Opener: 1 ♣
    Opener's rebid: 2 Notrump
15. Opener: 1 ♣
    Opener's rebid: 3 ◇
16. Opener: 1 ♣
    Opener's rebid: 3 ♣

CHAPTER 10

DOUBLES

A penalty double is a double of the opponents' final contract. This double enhances the premium which your side receives if you set the contract.

A take-out double is a double made after an opponent has opened the bidding. You make a take-out double at your first opportunity to bid, and this double shows an opening hand with support for the unbid suits.

Requirements for a take-out double

In order to make a take-out double, your hand must meet *all* of the following requirements:

1. The strength to open the bidding (13+ points).
2. At least three cards in each of the unbid suits.
3. No more than two cards in the opponents' suit.

Requirements for a penalty double

There are no particular requirements for making a penalty double. That double is made when, in your judgment, the opponents have bid too high, and you feel quite strongly that the opponents will fail to make their contract.

The chart below assumes the following:

1. That LHO* has opened the bidding with 1 of a suit.
2. That partner has doubled.
3. That RHO* has passed.

When the above occurs, respond as follows:

Responses to take-out doubles

Suit Responses

With 0-9 points ...... bid your longest suit as cheaply as possible.

With 10-12 points .... jump the bidding one level in your best suit.

With 13+ points ..... cue bid the opponents' suit.

Notrump Responses

With 7-10 HCPs and stoppers in the opponents' suit .... bid 1 Notrump

With 11-12 HCPs and stoppers in the opponents' suit .... bid 2 Notrump

With 13-15 HCPs and stoppers in the opponents' suit .... bid 3 Notrump

---

*LHO and RHO stand for left-hand opponent and right-hand opponent and will be used throughout this book when discussing opponents' bids.

RHO INTERVENES

The chart below assumes the following:

1. That LHO has opened the bidding with 1 of a suit.
2. That partner has doubled.
3. That RHO has then bid something other than Pass.

When the above occurs, respond as follows:

With 0-5 points ...... Pass
With 6-9 points ...... Bid your longest suit as cheaply as possible.

With other point ranges, respond exactly as set forth in the preceding chart.

REDOUBLES

---

1. When a contract has been doubled, a redouble increases again the premium that will be scored by the defending side if the contract is defeated or by the declaring side if the contract succeeds.
2. A far more common use of the redouble arises when your RHO doubles partner's opening suit bid. You respond as follows:

With 0-5 points ...... Pass
With 6-9 points ...... Raise partner's suit with support for that suit. Without support for partner's suit, bid your own suit as cheaply as possible.
With 10+points ...... Redouble

When partner opens and RHO doubles, any bid other than redouble promises less than 10 HCPs.

For each example below, select the appropriate bid.

1. You hold: ♠ 6
              ♡ Q J 9 7
              ◇ A K 9 4
              ♣ A 9 5 3

LHO	Partner	RHO	You
Pass	Pass	1♠	?

2. You hold: ♠ A Q J
              ♡ A K 8 6
              ◇ A 6 5 4
              ♣ 6 4

LHO	Partner	RHO	You
Pass	Pass	1♣	?

3. You hold: ♠ K Q 5 4
              ♡ K J 9 4
              ◇ 3
              ♣ A 9 7 2

LHO	Partner	RHO	You
1◇	Pass	Pass	?

4. You hold: ♠ 8 7 6
              ♡ 7 6 3
              ◇ 9 7 4
              ♣ 9 8 6 2

LHO	Partner	RHO	You
1♠	Double	Pass	?

5. You hold: ♠ 8 7 6
           ♡ 7 6 3
           ◊ 9 7 4
           ♣ 9 8 6 2

LHO	Partner	RHO	You
1 ♠	Double	1 NT	?

6. You hold: ♠ 5 4 3
           ♡ 6 4 2
           ◊ Q 9 8
           ♣ K Q J 7

LHO	Partner	RHO	You
1 ♠	Double	Pass	?

7. You hold: ♠ 8 7 4
           ♡ 7 4 2
           ◊ K Q 4
           ♣ K Q J 9

LHO	Partner	RHO	You
1 ♠	Double	Pass	?

8. You hold: ♠ 8 7 4
           ♡ 7 4 2
           ◊ K Q 4
           ♣ K Q J 9

LHO	Partner	RHO	You
1 ♣	Double	Pass	?

9. You hold: ♠ J 8 6
               ♡ K J 9 8
               ◇ K 4
               ♣ 6 5 4 2

LHO	Partner	RHO	You
1 ♡	Double	Pass	?

10. You hold: ♠ 8 5
               ♡ 8 4
               ◇ Q J 9 4
               ♣ A K 4 3 2

LHO	Partner	RHO	You
1 ♡	Double	Pass	?

11. You hold: ♠ 6
               ♡ K J 9 5
               ◇ K Q 4 3
               ♣ K Q 7 6

LHO	Partner	RHO	You
1 ♠	Double	Pass	?

12. You hold: ♠ K 5
               ♡ Q 6 5 4
               ◇ A 7 6 3
               ♣ Q 8 2

LHO	Partner	RHO	You
Pass	1 ♣	Double	?

ANSWERS TO QUIZ NO. 10

1. Double

2. Double

3. Double

4. 2♣

5. Pass

6. 2♣

7. 3♣

8. 2 Notrump

9. 1 Notrump

10. 3♣

11. 2♠

12. Redouble

CHAPTER 11

OVERCALLS

An opponent opens the bidding and it is your turn to bid. If you bid something other than pass or double, that bid is called an *overcall*.

Requirements to Overcall in a Suit

1. 10 or more high card points.
2. A suit at least five cards in length.

Responses to Overcalls in a Suit

WITH SUPPORT FOR PARTNER'S SUIT

1. 8 to 10 points . . raise partner's suit one level
2. 11 to 13 points . jump raise partner's suit
3. 14+ points . . . . cue bid the opponents' suit

WITHOUT SUPPORT FOR PARTNER'S SUIT

1. Bid a good five-card or longer suit of your own with 8 to 12 points.
2. With stoppers in the opponents' suit, bid:
   a. 1 Notrump with 8 to 10 high card points
   b. 2 Notrump with 11 to 13 high card points
   c. 3 Notrump with 14 to 16 high card points
   d. Cue bid the opponents' suit with 17+ high card points

Requirements to Overcall 1 Notrump

1. 16 to 18 high card points
2. A notrump pattern.
3. A stopper in the opponents' suit.

NOTE: In responding to an overcall of 1 Notrump, simply ignore the opponents' opening bid, and respond exactly as set forth in Chapter 8.

Jump overcalls are overcalls which skip a level of bidding. By agreement, jump overcalls may be played as weak, intermediate, or strong.

Requirements for Weak Jump Overcall

1. A suit at least 6 cards in length.
2. 6 to 11 points.

Requirements for an Intermediate Jump Overcall

1. A suit 6 or more cards in length.
2. 15 to 18 points.

Requirements for a Strong Jump Overcall

1. A suit 6 or more cards in length.
2. 19 to 21 points.

NOTE: With 22 or more points, do not make a jump overcall, even if you are playing strong jump overcalls. Instead, overcall with a cue bid of the opponents' suit, which tells partner that you would probably have opened with a strong 2 bid yourself had your opponent not opened in front of you.

For each of the following, determine your correct bid:

1. ♠ 6 5
   ♥ A K Q 6 4
   ♦ 9 6
   ♣ A 9 8 4

RHO	You
1 ♠	?

2. ♠ 3
   ♥ A K J 7 3
   ♦ Q 9 7 2
   ♣ 7 6 4

RHO	You
1 ♣	?

3. ♠ J 9 6
   ♥ 5 4
   ♦ A Q J 9 4
   ♣ A Q 4

RHO	You
1 ♠	?

4. ♠ —
   ♥ A Q J 10 5
   ♦ A K Q 8 6
   ♣ A Q 4

RHO	You
1 ♠	?

5. ♠ A Q
   ♡ K 6 5
   ◇ Q 5 4 3
   ♣ A Q 7 3

RHO	You
1♠	?

6. ♠ K 4
   ♡ 9 8 5 4 2
   ◇ A 3 2
   ♣ Q J 4

RHO	You
1◇	?

7. ♠ 8 7
   ♡ Q J 9 6
   ◇ 4 3 2
   ♣ K Q 9 5

LHO	Partner	RHO	You
1◇	1♡	Pass	?

8. ♠ K 9
   ♡ Q J 9 6
   ◇ 4 3 2
   ♣ K Q 9 5

LHO	Partner	RHO	You
1◇	1♡	Pass	?

9. ♠ K Q 8 5
   ♡ 3
   ◇ A J 7 5
   ♣ A 9 8 5

LHO	Partner	RHO	You
1♡	1♠	Pass	?

10. ♠ K 4
    ♡ Q J 9 5
    ◊ 10 8 6 3
    ♣ K 8 5

LHO	Partner	RHO	You
1 ♡	1 ♠	Pass	?

11. ♠ K 4
    ♡ J 4 3
    ◊ A Q 9 5
    ♣ A Q 5 2

LHO	Partner	RHO	You
1 ◊	1 ♠	Pass	?

12. ♠ Q J 10 6 4
    ♡ 3 2
    ◊ K 9 5
    ♣ K 8 7

LHO	Partner	RHO	You
1 ◊	1 ♡	Pass	?

13. ♠ K J 7 6
    ♡ K J 9 4
    ◊ 5 4
    ♣ Q 5 3

LHO	Partner	RHO	You
1 ◊	1 NT	Pass	?

WHEN YOU CONSIDER AN OVERCALL,
BALANCE THE RISK AGAINST THE
POSSIBLE GAIN FOR YOUR PARTNERSHIP.

1. 2 ♡

2. 1 ♡

3. 2 ♢

4. 2 ♠

5. 1 Notrump

6. Pass (Your suit is too weak to overcall 1 ♡)

7. 2 ♡

8. 3 ♡

9. 2 ♡

10. 1 Notrump

11. 3 Notrump

12. 1 ♠

13. 2 ♣ (Stayman)

CHAPTER 12

DECLARER PLAY

Advance planning is the key to successful declarer play. When the dummy comes down, do *not* simply start playing cards without a plan. Instead, form a plan of attack for each hand and try to carry it out. On some occasions you will adjust your plan as the play of the hand develops; however, you should not start playing any hand until you have formed a plan.

PLANNING THE PLAY IN SUIT CONTRACTS

When the dummy comes down and you are declaring a suit contract, ask yourself the following questions:

1. How many tricks must I win in order to fulfill my contract?

2. How many tricks am I in danger of losing? Is there any way to avoid those losers?

3. How many tricks can I win "off the top" with high cards such as Aces, Kings, and Queens?

4. Can I afford to draw trumps now, or do I need the trumps to ruff cards in the other suits?

PLANNING THE PLAY IN
NOTRUMP CONTRACTS

When the dummy comes down and you are playing a notrump contract, ask yourself the following questions:

1. How many tricks must I win in order to fulfill my contract?

2. How many tricks can I win "off the top" with high cards such as Aces, Kings, and Queens?

3. What suit or suits can I develop to provide additional tricks needed to make the contract?

    NOTE: At notrump, develop or set up the tricks you need in a long suit *before* taking the Aces and Kings you have in your other suits. If you take the Aces and Kings in the other suits first, your opponents will take additional tricks in those suits when you let them obtain the lead. Conversely, should the opponents attack a suit in which you have only one stopper, consider refusing to win that trick immediately (hold-up play).

QUIZ NO. 12

In working the following quizzes, it will be helpful to use a deck of cards. Spread out all four hands and plan the play in each contract.

In each of the following quizzes, assume that you are South, declarer, and that it is your job to make the contract. Good luck!

HAND 1:

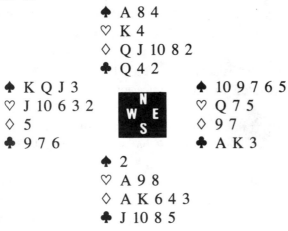

```
                    ♠ A 8 4
                    ♡ K 4
                    ◇ Q J 10 8 2
                    ♣ Q 4 2
    ♠ K Q J 3                      ♠ 10 9 7 6 5
    ♡ J 10 6 3 2         N         ♡ Q 7 5
    ◇ 5              W       E      ◇ 9 7
    ♣ 9 7 6              S          ♣ A K 3
                    ♠ 2
                    ♡ A 9 8
                    ◇ A K 6 4 3
                    ♣ J 10 8 5
```

The bidding:

South	West	North	East
1 ◇	Pass	3 ◇	Pass
5 ◇	Pass	Pass	Pass

Opening Lead: ♠ K

Play the above hand several times. Then answer each of the following questions:

1. Who is the declarer? _____

2. How many tricks do you need for your contract? _____

78

3. How many tricks can you take "off the top" with high cards? _____

4. What suit offers the best possibility for developing extra tricks? _____

5. Which hand will win the first trick? _____

6. Can you afford to draw trumps now? _____

7. State generally how you would play this hand as declarer.

_____

_____

_____

_____

_____

_____

8. How many tricks did you take? _____

9. How many tricks did you lose? _____

10. Did you make the contract? _____

HAND 2:

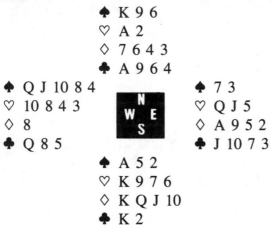

```
                    ♠ K 9 6
                    ♡ A 2
                    ◇ 7 6 4 3
                    ♣ A 9 6 4
      ♠ Q J 10 8 4         N         ♠ 7 3
      ♡ 10 8 4 3      W         E    ♡ Q J 5
      ◇ 8                 S         ◇ A 9 5 2
      ♣ Q 8 5                       ♣ J 10 7 3
                    ♠ A 5 2
                    ♡ K 9 7 6
                    ◇ K Q J 10
                    ♣ K 2
```

The bidding:

South	West	North	East
1 NT	Pass	3 NT	Pass
Pass	Pass		

Opening Lead: ♠ Q

Play the above hand several times. Then answer each of the following questions:

1. Who is the declarer? _____

2. How many tricks do you need for your contract? _____

3. How many tricks can you take "off the top" with high

   cards? _____

4. What suit offers the best possibility for developing extra

   tricks? _____

5. Which hand will win the first trick? _____

6. State generally how you would play this hand as declarer.

_____

_____

_____

_____

_____

_____

7. How many tricks did you take? _____

8. How many tricks did you lose? _____

9. Did you make the contract? _____

HAND 3:

<pre>
                    ♠ J 7 2
                    ♥ A 4 3
                    ◊ 8 5
                    ♣ K Q 9 8 3
        ♠ 8 6   ♠ Q 10 9 5 4
        ♥ Q J 10 5 2   N   ♥ 9 7
        ◊ 4 3 2   W   E   ◊ K Q 10 9
        ♣ A 10 2   S   ♣ 7 4
                    ♠ A K 3
                    ♥ K 8 6
                    ◊ A J 7 6
                    ♣ J 6 5
</pre>

The bidding:

South	West	North	East
1 NT	Pass	3 NT	Pass
Pass	Pass		

Opening Lead: ♥Q

Play the above hand several times. Then answer each of the following questions:

1. Who is the declarer? _____

2. How many tricks do you need for your contract? _____

3. How many tricks can you take "off the top" with high

   cards? _____

4. What suit offers the best possibility for developing extra

   tricks? _____

5. Which hand will win the first trick? _____

6. State generally how you would play this hand as declarer.

_____

_____

_____

_____

_____

_____

7. How many tricks did you take? _____

8. How many tricks did you lose? _____

9. Did you make the contract? __ _____

HAND 4:

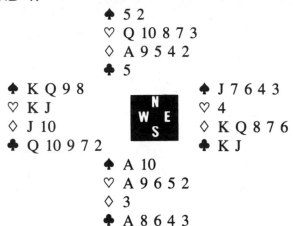

♠ 5 2
♡ Q 10 8 7 3
◇ A 9 5 4 2
♣ 5

♠ K Q 9 8   ♠ J 7 6 4 3
♡ K J   ♡ 4
◇ J 10   ◇ K Q 8 7 6
♣ Q 10 9 7 2   ♣ K J

♠ A 10
♡ A 9 6 5 2
◇ 3
♣ A 8 6 4 3

The bidding:

South	West	North	East
1 ♡	Pass	4 ♡	Pass
Pass	Pass		

Opening Lead: ♠ K

Play the above hand several times. Then answer each of the following questions:

1. Who is the declarer? _____

2. How many tricks do you need for your contract? _____

3. How many tricks can you take "off the top" with high

   cards? _____

4. What suit offers the best possibility for developing extra

   tricks? _____

5. Which hand will win the first trick? _____

6. Can you afford to draw any of the opponents' trumps?

   _____

7. State generally how you would play this hand as declarer.

   _____

   _____

   _____

   _____

   _____

   _____

8. How many tricks did you take? _____

9. How many tricks did you lose? _____

10. Did you make the contract? _____

11. How many tricks would you have won if you had begun play with two rounds of trumps? _____

HAND 5:

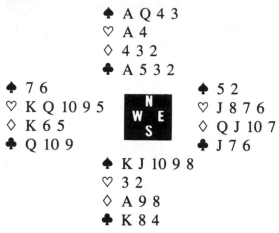

```
                    ♠ A Q 4 3
                    ♡ A 4
                    ◊ 4 3 2
                    ♣ A 5 3 2
   ♠ 7 6                              ♠ 5 2
   ♡ K Q 10 9 5         N            ♡ J 8 7 6
   ◊ K 6 5           W     E         ◊ Q J 10 7
   ♣ Q 10 9             S            ♣ J 7 6
                    ♠ K J 10 9 8
                    ♡ 3 2
                    ◊ A 9 8
                    ♣ K 8 4
```

The bidding:

South	West	North	East
		1 ♣	Pass
1 ♠	Pass	2 ♠	Pass
3 ♠	Pass	4 ♠	Pass
Pass	Pass		

Opening Lead: ♡ K

Play the above hand several times. Then answer each of the following questions:

1. Who is the declarer? _____

2. How many tricks do you need for your contract? _____

3. How many tricks can you take "off the top" with high

   cards? _____

4. What suit offers the best possibility for developing extra tricks? _____

5. Which hand will win the first trick? _____

6. Can you afford to draw trumps now? _____

7. State generally how you would play this hand as declarer.

_____

_____

_____

_____

_____

_____

8. How many tricks did you take? _____

9. How many tricks did you lose? _____

10. Did you make the contract? _____

HAND 6:

```
              ♠ 10 9 4 2
              ♡ K 9
              ◊ A K 9 5
              ♣ Q 6 4
   ♠ J 8 5                    ♠ Q 7 6 3
   ♡ 8 7 5 2       N          ♡ A 6
   ◊ 7 3        W   E         ◊ J 10 8 4
   ♣ A K 5 3       S          ♣ 8 7 2
              ♠ A K
              ♡ Q J 10 4 3
              ◊ Q 6 2
              ♣ J 10 9
```

The bidding:

South	West	North	East
1 ♡	Pass	1 ♠	Pass
1 NT	Pass	3 NT	Pass
Pass	Pass		

Opening Lead: ♣3

Play the above hand several times. Then answer each of the following questions:

1. Who is the declarer? _____

2. How many tricks do you need for your contract? _____

3. How many tricks can you take "off the top" with high

   cards? _____

4. What suit offers the best possibility for developing extra

   tricks? _____

5. Which hand will win the first trick? _____

6. State generally how you would play this hand as declarer.

_____

_____

_____

_____

_____

_____

7. How many tricks did you take? _____

8. How many tricks did you lose? _____

9. Did you make the contract? _____

HAND 7:

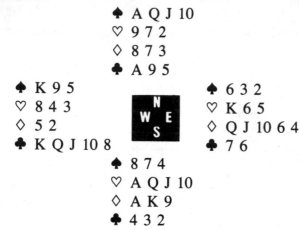

```
                    ♠ A Q J 10
                    ♡ 9 7 2
                    ◇ 8 7 3
                    ♣ A 9 5
    ♠ K 9 5                       ♠ 6 3 2
    ♡ 8 4 3            N          ♡ K 6 5
    ◇ 5 2          W     E        ◇ Q J 10 6 4
    ♣ K Q J 10 8      S           ♣ 7 6
                    ♠ 8 7 4
                    ♡ A Q J 10
                    ◇ A K 9
                    ♣ 4 3 2
```

The bidding:

South	West	North	East
1 ♣	Pass	1 ♠	Pass
1 NT	Pass	2 NT	Pass
3 NT	Pass	Pass	Pass

Opening Lead: ♣K

Play the above hand several times. Then answer each of the following questions:

1. Who is the declarer? _____

2. How many tricks do you need for your contract? _____

3. How many tricks can you take "off the top" with high

   cards? _____

4. What suit offers the best possibility for developing extra

   tricks? _____

5. Which hand will win the first trick? _____

6. State generally how you would play this hand as declarer.

   _____

   _____

   _____

   _____

   _____

   _____

7. How many tricks did you take? _____

8. How many tricks did you lose? _____

9. Did you make the contract? _____

HAND 8:

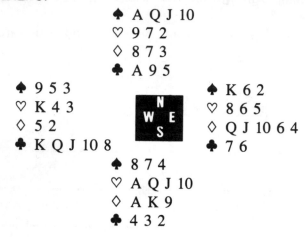

♠ A Q J 10
♡ 9 7 2
◊ 8 7 3
♣ A 9 5

♠ 9 5 3
♡ K 4 3
◊ 5 2
♣ K Q J 10 8

♠ K 6 2
♡ 8 6 5
◊ Q J 10 6 4
♣ 7 6

♠ 8 7 4
♡ A Q J 10
◊ A K 9
♣ 4 3 2

The bidding:

South	West	North	East
1 ♣	Pass	1 ♠	Pass
1 NT	Pass	2 NT	Pass
3 NT	Pass	Pass	Pass

Opening Lead: ♣K

Play the above hand several times. Then answer each of the following questions:

1. Who is the declarer? _____

2. How many tricks do you need for your contract? _____

3. How many tricks can you take "off the top" with high

   cards? _____

4. What suit offers the best possibility for developing extra

   tricks? _____

5. Which hand will win the first trick? _____

6. State generally how you would play this hand as declarer.

   _____

   _____

   _____

   _____

   _____

   _____

7. How many tricks did you take? _____

8. How many tricks did you lose? _____

9. Did you make the contract? _____

CONCENTRATION IS A VALUABLE ASSET
FOR THE DECLARER.

ANSWERS TO QUIZ NO. 12

HAND 1:
1. South
2. Eleven
3. Eight — Five diamond tricks; ace, king of hearts, and ace of spades.
4. Clubs. Also two small spades in the North hand can be trumped in the South hand.
5. North
6. Yes. It may be necessary to trump two spades in the South hand and one heart in the North hand. You have enough trumps to draw trumps and still ruff those cards as necessary.
7. Win the king of spades with the ace and draw two rounds of trumps, exhausting the opponents' trumps. Concede two club tricks to the ace and king of clubs, trump dummy's two spade losers in your hand, and trump South's heart loser in the dummy.
8. Eleven
9. Two
10. Yes

HAND 2:
1. South
2. Nine
3. Six
4. Diamonds
5. Either North or South is correct.
6. Win the opening lead and play diamonds. Continue playing diamonds until East takes the ace of diamonds. Win any return, and take three diamond tricks, two club tricks, two hearts, and two spades.
7. Nine
8. Four
9. Yes

HAND 3:
1. South
2. Nine
3. Five
4. Clubs
5. South
6. Win the queen of hearts in the South hand with the king. Lead a small club to the king. Assuming West has refused to play his ace on the first round of clubs, lead a small club from dummy to the jack in your hand. If West ducks again, lead a third club, forcing West to take his ace. Win any return, go to dummy with the ace of hearts, cash all the clubs, the ace, king of spades and the ace of diamonds.

    NOTE: If you had won the first trick with the ace of hearts in dummy instead of with the king in your hand, the opponents could have defeated you in 3 notrump. Try replaying the hand after winning the first heart trick with the ace. You will find that if West ducks two rounds of clubs, you will be cut off from the dummy and you will only make two clubs instead of the four club tricks to which you are entitled.
7. Nine
8. Four
9. Yes

HAND 4:
1. South
2. Ten
3. Four
4. None, but the trumps can be used separately to make tricks by cross-ruffing.
5. South
6. Yes. You can afford to draw one round of trumps with the Ace. You must leave four trumps remaining in each hand because you must try to ruff four losing clubs in the North hand and four losing diamonds in the South hand.

7. Win the ace of spades and cash the ace of hearts. Play the ace of clubs, then ruff a club in dummy. Play the ace of diamonds and ruff a diamond in the South hand. Continue playing clubs and trumping them in dummy followed by diamonds which you will trump in your hand.
8. Eleven
9. Two
10. Yes, with an overtrick
11. Only ten. Playing a second round of trumps would have taken an extra trump from both the North and South hands, costing you a trick.

HAND 5:

1. South
2. Ten
3. Nine (five spade tricks, one heart, one diamond and two clubs)
4. Clubs
5. North
6. Yes
7. Win the opening lead with the ace of hearts in dummy and play the ace of spades followed by a small spade to the king in the South hand. This will exhaust the opponents' trumps. Next, play the king of clubs, a club to the ace, and a third round of clubs. This play will exhaust all the opponents' clubs, and will leave you with a small club in the North hand which is good. Win whatever the opponents lead back (probably a diamond), cross to the dummy with a trump, and lead your thirteenth club, throwing a small diamond on it. Give up a diamond and then trump North's third diamond in the South hand.
8. Ten
9. Three
10. Yes

HAND 6:
1. South
2. Nine
3. Five
4. Hearts
5. South
6. Win the opening club lead. Play a heart to the king. If East ducks, play another heart, forcing East to take his ace. After East takes the ace of hearts, he should return a club and West will take three club tricks. After West has taken his three club tricks, win any return and take your hearts, spades and diamonds, which are now all high.
7. Nine
8. Four
9. Yes

HAND 7:
1. South
2. Nine
3. Five
4. Spades and Hearts
5. West (declarer should play low on the first two club tricks — hold up play)
6. Duck the king of clubs opening lead, permitting West to win. West will play the queen of clubs at trick two and you should duck again. Win the third club with the ace. Play a small heart from dummy, finessing the ten. Play a small spade from the South hand, finessing the ten of spades in dummy. Play another heart, repeating the heart finesse. Play a second spade and finesse the jack. Play another heart and the king will appear on your right. Win the ace of hearts and cash the queen. Play another spade and the king will appear on your left. Win the ace and cash the queen, throwing a small diamond from the South hand on the last spade. The last two cards in your hand are the ace and king of diamonds.

98

7. Eleven
8. Two
9. Yes, with two overtricks

HAND 8:
1. South
2. Nine
3. Five
4. Spades and Hearts
5. West (declarer should play low on the first two club tricks — hold-up play)
6. Duck the king of clubs opening lead, permitting West to win. West will play the queen of clubs at trick two and you should duck again. Win the third club with the ace. Play a small heart from dummy, finessing the ten. West will take his king and cash two more club tricks. West then leads a diamond. Win the ace. Play a spade toward dummy and finesse the ten. East wins with the king and returns a diamond. You win and take the remainder of the tricks.
7. Seven
8. Six
9. No.

Note how vividly the last two hands demonstrate the power of the finesse. The location of the opponents' key high cards is very important. In the last two examples, you can see that switching the king of hearts and king of spades changed the result dramatically. Instead of making 3 Notrump with two overtricks, 3 Notrump went down two tricks.

CHAPTER 13

DEFENSIVE PLAY

Good defensive play at bridge is difficult. In the boxes below, you will find some generalized rules to help you. You will also find that this chapter contains an inordinate number of quiz questions. The reason is that, from the defender's perspective, each hand is unique, and even similar hands may require different defense depending upon the bidding. It will help you greatly in your defensive play to work and rework the quiz questions in this chapter several times.

The principles below apply whether you are leading against a suit contract or against a notrump contract.

1. From a suit headed by a sequence of cards, for example, King, Queen, Jack, lead the highest ranking card (King).

2. Without a sequence, but with a suit containing four or more cards, lead fourth best. For example, from Q 10 5 3 2, lead the 3.

3. Lead low from three cards headed by an honor.

4. Lead high from three small cards (top of nothing).

5. With two cards in a suit, lead the higher card first, followed by the lower card.

Opening leads against notrump contracts

1. If partner has bid a suit, lead it.

2. If partner has not bid a suit, lead fourth-best from your longest and strongest suit, unless it is headed by a sequence (in which case, lead the top of the sequence.)

Opening leads against suit contracts

1. If partner has bid a suit, consider leading that suit.

2. With shortness in a suit other than the trump suit, consider leading that suit in an effort to obtain ruffs.

3. Consider leading a suit in which you have a sequence in order to force out declarer's high cards and develop tricks in that suit.

Signalling

1. The play of an unusually high card asks partner to lead or to continue leading that suit.

2. The play of a low card is discouraging, and asks partner to switch to another suit.

QUIZ NO. 13

Assume that you have decided to lead from each of the card combinations listed below. Determine which card is the correct card to lead and circle it. Your answer should be the same irrespective of whether you are defending against a suit contract or a notrump contract.

1. (Q) J 10 2
2. (K) Q J 9 3
3. (Q) J 10 9 5
4. (J) 10 9
5. (Q) J
6. K 8 (2)
7. Q 10 (4)
8. J 9 (3)
9. Q 10 4 (3)
10. Q 10 4 (3) 2
11. K J 9 (7)
12. K J 9 (7) 5 2
13. (8) 7 3
14. Q 7 (3)
15. (Q) J (3)
16. Q 10 3 (2)
17. (8) 3 2
18. (K) Q J 6
19. K (J) 10 9
20. (8) 3

102

21. You hold: ♠ 9 3
♡ Q 10 5 4 2
◇ 8 6 3
♣ Q 9 8

The bidding:

LHO	Partner	RHO	You
Pass	Pass	1 NT	Pass
3 NT	Pass	Pass	Pass

What is your opening lead? _____

22. You hold: ♠ 9 3
♡ Q 10 5 4 2
◇ 8 6 3
♣ Q 9 8

The bidding:

LHO	Partner	RHO	You
Pass	1 ♠	1 NT	Pass
3 NT	Pass	Pass	Pass

What is your opening lead? _____

23. You hold: ♠ J 6 4
♡ Q J 10 7 5
◇ 3
♣ Q 10 5 2

The bidding:

LHO	Partner	RHO	You
		1 NT	Pass
3 NT	Pass	Pass	Pass

What is your opening lead? _____

24. You hold: ♠ J 6 4
♡ Q J 8 7 5
◊ 3
♣ Q 10 5 ②

The bidding:

LHO	Partner	RHO	You
		1 ♡	Pass
1 ♠	Pass	1 NT	Pass
3 NT	Pass	Pass	Pass

What is your opening lead? _____

25. You hold: ♠ J 6 4
♡ Q J 10 7 5
◊ ③
♣ Q 10 5 2

The bidding:

LHO	Partner	RHO	You
		1 ♠	Pass
3 ♠	Pass	4 ♠	Pass
Pass	Pass		

What is your opening lead? _____

26.

```
              ♠ A 9 8
              ♡ Q 8
              ◇ K 10 5 4 3
              ♣ Q 7 6
  ♠ 10 5 4              ♠ Q 6 3 2
  ♡ J 10 9 7 3    N     ♡ K 4 2
  ◇ 9 2         W   E   ◇ Q J 8 7
  ♣ A 8 2         S     ♣ 4 3
              ♠ K J 7
              ♡ A 6 5
              ◇ A 6
              ♣ K J 10 9 5
```

Look at the hand above and assume that you hold the West cards. Assume that South opens 1 Notrump, you pass, and North bids 3 Notrump, ending the auction. Answer the following questions:

A. What is your opening lead? _____ J H _____

B. What card should South play from dummy? ___ Q H ___

C. What card should East play at trick 1? ___ K H ___

Who will win the first trick? _____ E _____

D. What should East lead at the second trick?___ 4 H ___

E. Assuming South plays low at trick 2, who will win this

trick? _____ W _____

F. What suit should West lead at trick 3? ___ H ___

G. How many tricks can South take off the top?___ 5 ___

H. In order to make his contract, what suit must South develop? _C_ _____

I. When South leads clubs, what should West do?

_____ A c + H 9 _____

_____

J. Did South make his contract? _No_____

27.

```
              ♠ A Q 9 8
              ♡ 10
              ◇ A K 9 6 5
              ♣ J 10 2
♠ 10 7 3                        ♠ 5 4 2
♡ Q 7 6 4         N            ♡ J 9 8 5 3 2
◇ 4           W       E        ◇ J 2
♣ K Q 9 8 5       S            ♣ A 6
              ♠ K J 6
              ♡ A K
              ◇ Q 10 8 7 3
              ♣ 7 4 3
```

Look at the hands above and assume that you hold the West cards. Assume that South opens 1 ◇, you pass, North bids 1 ♠, East passes, South bids 1 NT, you pass, North bids 3 ◇, East passes, and South bids 5 ◇, ending the auction. Answer the following questions:

A. What is your opening lead? ___K C___

B. What card should East play to the first trick? ___A C___

_____

Why? ___set up ruff at trick 3___

C. After East wins the ace of clubs at the first trick what

should East return? ___6 C___

D. What should West play at the second trick? ___Q C___

E. What should West lead at trick 3? ___5 C___

Why? ___Ruff / set ruff.___

F. Did South make his contract? ___N O___

107

DEFENSE IS THE MOST CHALLENGING
PART OF BRIDGE.

ANSWERS TO QUIZ NO. 13

1. Queen
2. King
3. Queen
4. Jack
5. Queen
6. Two
7. Four
8. Three
9. Three
10. Three
11. Seven
12. Seven
13. Eight
14. Three
15. Queen
16. Two
17. Eight
18. King
19. Jack
20. Eight
21. Four of Hearts
22. Nine of Spades
23. Queen of Hearts
24. Two of Clubs
25. Three of Diamonds
26. A. Jack of Hearts
    B. Queen of Hearts
    C. King of Hearts; East
    D. Four of Hearts
    E. West
    F. Hearts
    G. Five
    H. Clubs. The club suit will produce four tricks after the ace is knocked out.

I. Play the ace of clubs and cash the remaining two heart tricks.

J. No. The defense took four heart tricks and the ace of clubs, and South went down one.

27. A. King of Clubs

B. Ace of Clubs. If East does not play the ace, West will lead another club and East will win. East will not be able to lead any more clubs. Declarer will win any other suit that East returns and play the ace and king of hearts, throwing the remaining club loser from the dummy.

C. Six of Clubs.

D. Queen of Clubs, which will win the trick.

E. Another club. North and South will have to follow suit to the third club and East will play a diamond, trumping the trick.

F. No. The contract was defeated, as the defense took the first three tricks.

Note that East and West must start the defense by playing three rounds of clubs. If East and West defend in any other way, South will make five diamonds.

CHAPTER 14

SLAM BIDDING

To bid slam, you must bid at the six level (small slam) or at the seven level (grand slam). The partnership must take twelve tricks to make a small slam and must bid and make all thirteen tricks to achieve a grand slam.

Requirements to bid a small slam

1. The partnership should possess 33 or more points.

2. The partnership must have first- or second-round control in each suit. Otherwise, you may lose the first two tricks.

Requirements to bid a grand slam

1. The partnership should possess 37 or more points.

2. The partnership must have first-round control in all suits. Otherwise, you may lose the first trick.

The Blackwood Convention

4 Notrump .... Asks for Aces

Responses to 4 Notrump

5 ♣ .... No Aces or all four Aces
5 ♦ .... One Ace
5 ♡ .... Two Aces
5 ♠ .... Three Aces

5 Notrump .... Guarantees that the partnership has all four Aces and asks for Kings

Responses to 5 Notrump

6 ♣ .... No Kings
6 ♦ .... One King
6 ♡ .... Two Kings
6 ♠ .... Three Kings
6 Notrump .... Four Kings

If you initiate Blackwood and discover that you are missing two Aces, you may sign off by bidding five of the agreed trump suit. You may also sign off by bidding five of a new suit, which asks partner to bid 5 NT.

1. How many tricks must your side take in order to make a small slam? _____

2. How many tricks must your side take in order to make a grand slam? _____

3. How many points should you and partner possess together in order to have a reasonable expectation of making a small slam? _____

4. How many points should you and partner possess together in order to have a reasonable expection of making a grand slam? _____

5. A bid of 4 Notrump is the _____ Convention.

6. A response of 5 ♡ to a Blackwood 4 Notrump shows _____ Aces.

7. After partner has responded to your 4 Notrump inquiry, a bid of 5 Notrump guarantees that the partnership possesses _____ Aces.

8. Five Notrump asks partner to tell you the number of _____ he holds.

9. After partner responds to your 4 Notrump inquiry, and you follow up with 5 Notrump, a 6 ◊ response by partner shows _____.

10.

```
              ♠ A 8 5
              ♡ Q J 6 3
              ◇ 6 5 4
              ♣ A Q 9
  ♠ Q J 10 6              ♠ 7 4 3 2
  ♡ 8 7          N        ♡ 9
  ◇ Q 7 2      W   E      ◇ 10 9 3
  ♣ J 6 5 4      S        ♣ K 10 8 3 2
              ♠ K 9
              ♡ A K 10 5 4 2
              ◇ A K J 8
              ♣ 7
```

On the hand shown above, assume that you are South.

A. How many points does the South hand contain? _____21_____

B. How many points does the North hand contain? _____13_____

C. What is the combined total of points between the North and South hands? _____34_____

D. What is your opening bid? _____1 H_____

E. What will North respond? _____3 H_____

F. What should you do next? _____4 N_____

_____Blackwood._____

_____

_____

G. What is North's proper response? _____4 S_____

H. What should South bid next? _____4 N_____

I. What is North's proper response? _____5 H_____

5 N
6 C
6 H

115

J. What should you bid now? _____

K. What should West lead? _____

L. State generally how South should play the hand.

_____

_____

_____

_____

_____

M. Did you make the contract? _____

N. What trick or tricks did you lose? _____

_____

_____

1, 12
2. 13
3. 33 or more
4. 37 or more
5. Blackwood
6. Two
7. Four
8. Kings
9. 1 King
10. A. 21
  B. 13
  C. 34
  D. 1♡
  E. 3♡
  F. Bid 4 Notrump, Blackwood, asking for Aces
  G. 5♡
  H. 5 Notrump, asking for Kings
  I. 6♣, no Kings
  J. 6♡ (small slam in Hearts)
  K. Queen of Spades
  L. Win the opening spade lead in either hand and draw trump in 2 rounds. Play the ace of diamonds, cross to dummy, and lead a diamond to the jack. The finesse loses to the queen. That is the only trick you should lose.
  M. Yes
  N. The only trick lost was to the queen of diamonds.

CHAPTER 15

FINAL EXAM

This quiz contains 100 review questions covering all aspects of beginning bridge. To rate your knowledge and progress, take the exam without looking back at any of the preceding chapters for help. After you complete the exam, check your answers. If you miss a question, refer to the chapter indicated following the answer for further review.

Please remember that the referenced chapter numbers are identical for both *Beginning Bridge Quizzes* and *Beginning Bridge Complete*. Therefore, if you look back at the appropriate chapter of *Beginning Bridge Quizzes* but would like a more in-depth review of the subject matter, please refer to the same numbered chapter of *Beginning Bridge Complete*.

1. You hold: ♠ 9 ♡ A J 10 3 2 ◇ K 8 6 3 ♣ Q 9 7
   a. How many high-card points do you hold?_____
   b. How many distributional points do you hold? _____
   c. What is the total value of this hand? _____

2. To have a reasonable expectation of making a small slam, a partnership should have a combined total of at least how many points? _____

3. A bid of 4 NT asks partner to tell you the number of _____ he holds. This bid is an example of the _____ convention.

4. You hold ♠ 8 2. If you choose to lead this suit against any contract, which is the proper card to lead?
   _____

5. You hold: ♠ K 9 3 2   ♡ Q 10 8 5   ◇ A J 4 3   ♣ 5
   Partner opens 1 NT. What is your response? _____

6. You hold: ♠ A K J 10 5   ♡ A Q 9 3   ◇ A K J   ♣ 3
   What is your opening bid? _____

7. You hold: ♠ 7 3   ♡ K Q J 4 3   ◇ A 4   ♣ 9 6 3 2
   Partner passes and RHO opens 1 ◇. What is your bid?
   _____

8. Your partnership reaches a final contract of 3 ♣ and takes
   nine tricks. How many points do you score? _____
   Are the points scored above or below the line? _____

9. You hold: ♠ A 5 3 2   ♡ K J 3   ◇ K Q   ♣ 10 9 5 3
   What is your opening bid? _____

10. You hold: ♠ Q 10 2   ♡ A J 9 4   ◇ J 9 3   ♣ A K J
    What is your opening bid? _____

11. You are declarer. Before beginning play, whether at a
    suit or a notrump contract, what is the first question you
    should ask yourself? _____
    _____

12. You hold: ♠ 8   ♡ Q J 8 3   ◇ A J 9 4   ♣ K Q 7 5
    RHO deals and opens 1 ♠. What is your bid? _____

13. You hold: ♠ 3 2   ♡ 9 4   ◇ K Q 3   ♣ A Q J 10 4 3
    You open 1 ♣ and partner responds 1 ♠. What is your
    rebid? _____

14. You hold: ♠ Q 3 2   ♡ 9 7   ◇ A 6 3 2   ♣ J 8 7 4
    Partner opens 1 ♠. What is your response? _____

15. Which suit is higher-ranking, Diamonds or Clubs?
    _____

16. You hold: ♠ A 5 3 ♡ K 2 ◊ K 9 7 3 2 ♣ A 10 3
Partner opens 1 ◊ and you respond 3 ◊. Next partner bids
4 NT (Blackwood) and you respond 5 ◊ (1 Ace). Partner thens bids 5 NT. What is your response?

_____

17. How many games must your side win in order to earn
a rubber? _____

18. You hold: ♠ K 8 2
Partner leads the ace of spades. You decide that you want
partner to lead spades again. Which card should you
play? _____

19. You hold: ♠ A Q 9 3 2 ♡ 10 5 ◊ K Q 3 2 ♣ K 5
What is your opening bid? _____

20. You hold: ♠ K J 2 ♡ Q 5 ◊ K J 3 2 ♣ A 6 4 3
Partner opens 1 ♡. What is your response? _____

21. You hold: ◊ 3 2   Dummy holds: ◊ A Q
You lead the two of diamonds towards dummy. LHO
plays low. Which card should you play? _____
This play is called a _____ .

22. You hold: ♠ 4 ♡ 4 3 2 ◊ K Q J 9 7 5 3 ♣ 8 2
What is your opening bid? _____

23. You hold: ♠ 8 7 ♡ A Q 2 ◊ 10 8 3 2 ♣ K 7 6 4
LHO opens 1 ♡ and partner overcalls 1 ♠. RHO passes.
What is your bid?_____

24. You hold: ♠ K Q 2 ♡ A K J 3 ◊ K J 5 2 ♣ A Q
What is your opening bid? _____

25. Name the two major suits. _____

26. You hold: ♠ K 5 2   ♡ Q 3   ◇ A 9 7 4   ♣ J 10 3 2
    Partner opens 1 ♡. RHO doubles. What is your bid?

    _____

27. A game bid in hearts is _____ . A game bid
    in diamonds is _____ .

28. You hold: ♠ 6   ♡ J 10 6 4 3 2   ◇ Q 5   ♣ 10 8 4 3
    Partner opens 1 NT. What is your response? _____

29. You hold: ♠ K Q J 8 3   ♡ A J 2   ◇ 5   ♣ A K 4 2
    You open 1 ♠. Partner responds 2 ♠. What is your
    bid?_____

30. You hold: ♠ Q 9 4   ♡ K J 3   ◇ J 3 2   ♣ K J 8 5
    Partner opens 1 NT. What is your response? _____

31. You bid 4 NT (Blackwood) asking for Aces. Partner
    responds. If you now bid 5 NT, asking for Kings, you
    promise partner that the partnership holds how many
    Aces? _____

32. A void is worth _____ points.

33. True or False. The dealer bids first. _____

34. You hold: ♠ 6 4 3 and decide to lead spades. Which card
    should you lead? _____

35. The opponents are vulnerable and bid 3 ♠. You double
    and the opponents go down two tricks. How many points
    do you score? _____

36. True or False. Clubs and Diamonds are major
    suits. _____

37. True or False. In most suit contracts, it is a good idea to draw the opponents' trumps as soon as possible.

_____

38. You hold: ♠ A 8 3 2 ♡ K Q 3 ◇ A 8 7 ♣ 4 3 2
What is your opening bid? _____

39. You hold: ♠ K 5 3 ♡ A Q 9 ◇ K J 8 ♣ K J 7 2
RHO deals and opens 1♡. What is your bid? _____

40. You hold: ♠ A Q 5 ♡ K J 2 ◇ A K Q 3 ♣ A Q J
What is your opening bid? _____

41. How many points should your partnership hold to have a reasonable expectation of making 5♣ or 5◇? _____

42. How many tricks must you take in order to make a grand slam? _____

43. You hold: ♠ K J 2 ♡ A Q 10 ◇ J 3 2 ♣ K 6 5 3
LHO opens 1♡ and partner doubles. What is your response? _____

44. You hold: ♠ 5 4 3 ♡ J 3 2 ◇ K 7 6 2 ♣ 7 5 4
Partner opens 1♣. What is your response? _____

45. You hold: ♠ 5 4 2 ♡ J 3 2 ◇ K 7 6 2 ♣ 7 5 4
Partner opens 2♣. What is your response? _____

46. You hold: ♠ J 9 2 ♡ Q 4 2 ◇ 10 5 4 2 ♣ K 10 5
Partner opens 1 NT. What is your response? _____

47. You hold: ♠ J 9 2 ♡ Q 4 2 ◇ 10 5 4 2 ♣ K 10 5
Partner opens 2 NT. What is your response? _____

48. You hold: ♠ 5 4   ♡ A 9 2   ◇ K 8   ♣ A K J 9 6 2
    You open 1♣ and partner responds 1◇. What is your rebid? _____

49. True or False. 4♣ is a game bid in Clubs. _____

50. True or False. Down one, not doubled, not vulnerable scores 50 points. _____

51. You hold: ♠ Q 10 7 5 3   ♡ K Q 5   ◇ 6 2   ♣ Q 5 4
    RHO opens 1 NT, you pass, LHO bids 3 NT. What is your opening lead? _____

52. You hold: ♡ K Q J 7 2 and decide to lead hearts. Which is the correct card to lead? _____

53. You hold: ♠ K J 9 3 2   ♡ K J 9 3 2   ◇ A 5   ♣ 2
    What is your opening bid? _____

54. You hold: ♠ 4 3   ♡ Q 10 4 2   ◇ 7 4 2   ♣ A K Q 3
    LHO opens 1◇, partner bids 1♡, and RHO passes. What is your response? _____

55. You hold: ♠ 9 3 2   ♡ A Q J 6 3   ◇ J 5   ♣ K 6 4
    Partner opens 1 NT. What is your response? _____

56. You hold: ♠ J 3 2   ♡ 10 5 4   ◇ Q 4 3   ♣ K J 9 7
    Partner opens 1◇. What is your response? _____

57. You hold: ♠ K Q 2   ♡ 8 2   ◇ A Q J 3   ♣ A K 9 2
    You open 1◇. Partner responds 1♡. What is your rebid? _____

58. True or False. After someone opens the bidding, three consecutive passes will end the auction. _____

59. You hold: ♠ A J 3 2   ♡ K J 9 3   ◇ A 9 7   ♣ 10 3
Partner opens 3♣. What is your response? _____

60. You hold: ♠ K 5   ♡ A Q 9 4   ◇ 5 3 2   ♣ 9 7 3 2
Partner opens 1 ◇. What is your response? _____

61. True or False. A small slam bid in notrump is 6 NT, and requires the taking of 12 tricks. _____

62. You hold: ♠ 4   ♡ K 10 3 2   ◇ A 9 7 5 2   ♣ J 10 3
Partner opens 1 NT. What is your response? _____

63. You hold: ♠ A 10 5 4   ♡ 9   ◇ A Q 5 2   ♣ A Q 5 2
What is your opening bid? _____

64. You hold: ♠ K 2   ♡ A K 9 5 3   ◇ A Q 10 2   ♣ A 8
You open 1 ♡ and partner responds 3♡. What is your rebid? _____

65. You hold: ♠ 4   ♡ A 10 9 7   ◇ A Q 6 2   ♣ Q 9 8 5
LHO opens 1 ♠, partner passes, and RHO passes. What is your bid? _____

66. If you are declarer, you must win six tricks before you can start counting tricks towards your contract. Winning these six tricks is called making _____ .

67. You hold ♣ K 5 2. If you decide to lead a club, what is the correct card to lead from this holding? _____

68. What are the five honor cards in each suit? _____

69. You hold: ♠ K 4 2   ♡ J 3   ◇ J 6 4   ♣ K 9 6 4 3
Partner opens 1 ◇. What is your response? _____

70. You hold: ♠ A K 9 7 2   ♡ Q 8 3   ◊ 6   ♣ A 6 3 2
You open 1♠ and partner responds 2♠. What is your rebid? _____

71. You hold: ♠ J 5 3 2   ♡ A K 2   ◊ A Q 3 2   ♣ Q 9
You open 1 NT and partner responds 2♣. What is your rebid? _____

72. You hold: ♠ 5 4 3 2   ♡ 8 5 4   ◊ 6 4 3   ♣ 9 8 2
LHO deals and opens 1◊. Partner doubles and RHO passes. What is your bid? _____

73. True or False. 3 NT is a game bid in notrump. _____

74. You hold: ♠ 9 3   ♡ 5   ◊ A J 9 6 3   ♣ A K Q 8 7
What is your opening bid? _____

75. You hold: ♠ A Q 10 ♡ A K Q ◊ K Q 10 9 ♣ A Q 2
What is your opening bid? _____

76. You hold: ♠ 8 6 3   ♡ A 9   ◊ A K J 9 2   ♣ K 7 3
RHO deals and opens 1♠. What is your bid? _____

77. True or False. It's permissable to help partner decide what to play by winking, waving and shaking your head.

_____

78. What is the bonus for making a small slam, not vulnerable? _____

79. What is the highest level to which your partnership can bid? _____

80. True or False. Clubs are higher-ranking than Hearts.

_____

81. A response of 6 ◇ to a Blackwood 5 NT shows how many Kings? _____

82. You hold: ♠ K 6 3 2   ♡ A 5 4   ◇ 3 2   ♣ A Q 10 2
    You open 1 ♣ and partner responds 1 ♠. What is your rebid? _____

83. You hold ♣ Q J 10 7 4. If you choose to lead clubs, which is the correct card? _____

84. You hold: ♠ K 3 2   ♡ 9 5   ◇ 5 4 2   ♣ A K 9 7 4
    Partner deals and opens 1 ♠. What is your response?
    _____

85. You hold: ♠ K 10 3 2   ♡ A J 10 2   ◇ A K J 2   ♣ 8
    RHO deals and opens 3 ♣. What is your bid? _____

86. You hold: ♠ A Q J 10 8 7 5   ♡ 9 2   ◇ 8   ♣ 8 6 5
    What is your opening bid? _____

87. You hold: ♠ Q J 9 8 2   ♡ 9 8 5   ◇ K J   ♣ A 5 2
    RHO deals and opens 1 ◇. What is your bid? _____

88. The opponents bid 4 ♠, vulnerable. You double and they go down three tricks. How many points do you score?
    _____

89. You hold: ♠ A 10 3 2   ♡ K J 5 4   ◇ 5 3 2   ♣ A J
    What is your opening bid? _____

90. You hold: ♠ 8 6 5 3 2   ♡ 9   ◇ A K Q J 8   ♣ A 3
    What is your opening bid? _____

91. You hold: ♠ A J 3   ♡ K 5 4   ◇ A 6 5   ♣ A J 5 2
    You open 1 NT. Partner responds 2 ♣. What is your rebid?_____

92. You hold: ♠ 9 8 3　♡ 5 4 2　◇ 7 5 3 2　♣ 6 4 3
LHO deals and opens 1 ◇. Partner doubles. RHO bids
1 ♡. What is your bid?_____

93. You hold: ◇ J 10 9 5 3. You decide to lead a diamond.
Which card is correct? _____

94. You hold: ♠ A ♡ A K J ◇ A K Q 10 3 ♣ Q 10 9 3
What is your opening bid? _____

95. You hold: ♠ K J 8 6 3　♡ 5 4 2　◇ 6 2　♣ 6 5 2
Partner opens 1 NT. What is your response? _____

96. You hold: ♠ J 10 3　♡ K 2　◇ A J 9 2　♣ A 9 3 2
You open 1 ◇, partner responds 1 ♡. What is your rebid?

_____

97. You hold: ♠ A 3 2　♡ K 9 7　◇ K 7 6 3　♣ A 9 8
Partner deals and opens 1 ♣. What is your response?

_____

98. You hold: ♠ 9　♡ J 2　◇ K J 6 4 2　♣ Q 7 6 3 2
Partner opens 1 ◇. What is your response? _____

99. What is the score for 7 NT, doubled and redoubled,
vulnerable, making seven? _____

100. True or False. Bridge is the world's GREATEST card
game. _____

ANSWERS TO QUIZ CHAPTER 15

1. a. 10 (Chapter 1)
   b. 2
   c. 12
2. 33 points (Chapter 6)
3. Aces; Blackwood (Chapter 14)
4. 8 (Chapter 13)
5. 2♣ (Stayman) (Chapter 8)
6. 2♠ (Chapter 14)
7. 1♡ (Chapter 11)
8. 60; below the line (Chapter 2)
9. 1♣ (Chapter 3)
10. 1 NT (Chapter 5)
11. "How many tricks must I win in order to fulfill my contract?" (Chapter 12)
12. Double (Chapter 10)
13. 2♣ (Chapter 9)
14. 2♠ (Chapter 7)
15. Diamonds (Chapter 1)
16. 6♡ (Chapter 14)
17. 2 (Chapter 2)
18. 8 (Chapter 13)
19. 1♠ (Chapter 3)
20. 2 NT (Chapter 7)
21. Queen; Finesse (Chapter 12)
22. 3◇ (Chapter 4)
23. 1 NT (Chapter 11)
24. 2 NT (Chapter 5)
25. Spades and Hearts (Chapter 1)
26. Redouble (Chapter 10)
27. 4♡; 5◇ (Chapter 6)
28. 2♡ (Chapter 8)
29. 4♠ (Chapter 9)
30. 3 NT (Chapter 8)
31. 4 (all) (Chapter 14)
32. 3 (Chapter 1)

33. True (Chapter 1)
34. 6 (Chapter 13)
35. 500 (Chapter 2)
36. False (Chapter 1)
37. True (Chapter 12)
38. 1♣ (Chapter 3)
39. 1 NT (Chapter 11)
40. 3 NT (Chapter 5)
41. 29 (Chapter 6)
42. 13 (Chapter 6)
43. 3 NT (Chapter 10)
44. Pass (Chapter 7)
45. 2 NT (Chapter 7)
46. Pass (Chapter 8)
47. 3 NT (Chapter 8)
48. 3♣ (Chapter 9)
49. False (Chapter 6)
50. True (Chapter 2)
51. Five of Spades (Chapter 13)
52. King (Chapter 13)
53. 1♠ (Chapter 3)
54. 3♡ (Chapter 11)
55. 3♡ (Chapter 8)
56. 1 NT (Chapter 7)
57. 2 NT (Chapter 9)
58. True (Chapter 1)
59. Pass (Chapter 7)
60. 1♡ (Chapter 6)
61. True (Chapter 6)
62. 2♣ (Stayman) (Chapter 8)
63. 1♢ (Chapter 3)
64. 4 NT, Blackwood (Chapters 6 & 14)
65. Double (Chapter 10)
66. Book (Chapter 1)
67. 2 (Chapter 13)
68. A K Q J 10 (Chapter 2)
69. 1 NT (Chapter 7)

70. Pass (Chapter 9)
71. 2♠ (Chapter 8)
72. 1♠ (Chapter 10)
73. True (Chapter 6)
74. 1♢ (Chapter 3)
75. 3 NT (Chapter 5)
76. 2♢ (Chapter 11)
77. False (Chapter 13)
78. 500 points (Chapter 2)
79. The seven level (Chapter 1)
80. False (Chapter 1)
81. One (Chapter 14)
82. 2♠ (Chapter 9)
83. Q (Chapter 13)
84. 2♣ (Chapter 7)
85. Double (Chapter 10)
86. 3♠ (Chapter 4)
87. 1♠ (Chapter 11)
88. 800 (Chapter 2)
89. 1♢ (Chapter 3)
90. 1♠ (Chapter 3)
91. 2♢ (Chapter 8)
92. Pass (Chapter 10)
93. Jack (Chapter 13)
94. 2♢ (Chapter 4)
95. 2♠ (Chapter 8)
96. 1 NT (Chapter 9)
97. 2 NT (Chapter 7)
98. 2♢ (Chapter 7)
99. Far too much to count.
100. TRUE!

RESULTS

90 to 100 correct —	Excellent! You've mastered the principles of beginning bridge.
80 to 89 correct —	Superior. You have a good grasp of beginning bridge.
70 to 79 correct —	Good. You have good understanding of the basics.
60 to 69 correct —	Fair. You need to review the basics again.
50 to 59 correct —	Reread *Beginning Bridge Complete* and *Beginning Bridge Quizzes* and they try this test again.
Less than 50 correct —	Perhaps you should try Old Maid.

GLOSSARY OF TERMS

above the line—All scores entered above the horizontal line on the score sheet, including penalties and other bonuses.

auction—Bidding by the four players for the contract.

balancing—Reopening with a bid or double when the opposing bidding has stopped at a low level.

below the line—All scores entered below the horizontal line on the score sheet; only those points for bidding and making part-scores or games.

bid—A call by a player in the auction.

Blackwood Convention—Bid to determine the number of aces and kings in partner's hand; initiated with a bid of four notrump.

book—For the declarer, the first six tricks taken.

call—Any bid, double, redouble, or pass.

cash—To play a winning card and win the trick.

contract—The undertaking by declarer's side to win a specified number of tricks; the final bid in any auction.

controls—Holdings that prevent the opponents' winning one or two immediate tricks in a specified suit; aces and kings, or voids and singletons in side suits at suit contracts.

cue bid—A bid in a suit in which the bidder cannot wish to play the contract.

deal—To distribute the cards to the four players.

declarer—The player who first bid the denomination of the final bid; the person who plays the hand.

defender—An opponent of the declarer; one who attempts to prevent the declarer from making his contract.

denomination—The suit or notrump specified in a bid.

discard—To play a card which is neither of the suit led nor of the trump suit; the card so played.

distributional points—Points added to the value of your hand for shortness in one or more suits.

double—A call that increases the scoring value of an opponent's bid.

doubleton—A holding of two cards in a suit.

down—Defeated; a declarer who has failed to make his contract.

drawing trumps—The action of removing the trumps from the opponents' hands.

dummy—Declarer's partner; dummy's cards are placed face up on the table and played by declarer.

establish—To make a suit or specific card good by forcing out the opponent's winner(s).

extra trick—Overtrick; a trick scored in excess of the number of tricks required to fulfill a contract.

finesse—An attempt to win an extra trick or tricks for your side based on the favorable location of your opponents' cards.

fulfilling the contract—Taking as many tricks in the play of hand as contracted for in addition to book; for example, nine tricks in a contract of three.

game—Contract of 3 Notrump, 4 Hearts, 4 Spades, 5 Clubs or 5 Diamonds; the winning of 100 points below the line.

go down—fail to make a contract.

grand slam—Bidding and winning all 13 tricks by the declarer.

hand—The 13 cards held by any player in a bridge game.

high-card points (HCPs)—Points assigned to aces, kings, queens and jacks.

hold-up play—Refusing to win a trick at the first opportunity.

holding—The cards a player is dealt in a particular suit.

honor—Ace, king, queen, jack or 10.

invitation—A bid which encourages the bidder's partner to continue to game or slam, but gives him the option of passing with minimum values.

jump overcall—An overcall which skips a level of bidding.

jump raise—A bid which raises partner's suit two levels of bidding.

LHO—Left-hand opponent.

lead—The first card played to a trick.

major suits—Spades and hearts.

minor suits—Diamonds and clubs.

notrump—The highest denomination in the bidding; contracts that are played without a trump suit.

notrump distribution—A balanced hand; one which contains no void or singleton; usually 4-3-3-3, 4-4-3-2, or 5-3-3-2.

non-vulnerable—A side that has not won a game in a rubber.

opening bid—The first call in the auction other than a pass.

opening lead—After the bidding has been concluded, the first lead made by declarer's LHO.

overtricks—Tricks won by the declaring side in excess of those required to make a particular contract.

part-score (or partial)—Any contract below game level.

penalty double—Double of the opponents' contract made with the intention of setting that contract.

preemptive bid—An opening bid at the three-level or higher, containing a long suit and limited high-card strength.

redouble—A call that multiplies the doubled penalty or bonus by two.

response—First bid by the partner of the opening bidder.

reverse—A rebid at the two-level or more, in a higher-ranking suit than that bid originally; for example; 1♣ - 1♠ - 2♡ or 1♡ - 2♢ - 2♠.

RHO—Right-hand opponent.

rubber—Unit of bridge scoring achieved by winning two out of three games.

ruff—Play a trump in a suit in which the player is void.

Rule of Eleven—Calculation to determine the number of cards in declarer's hand higher than the fourth-best lead made by partner.

sequence—Cards in consecutive order, such as K-Q-J or J-10-9.

set—The failure of a contract; to defeat a contract.

side suit—Any suit other than the trump suit.

sign-off bid—Bid intended to end the auction, requesting partner to pass.

singleton—A holding of only one card in a suit.

small slam—Bidding and winning 12 tricks by the declarer.

spot card—2, 3, 4, 5, 6, 7, 8, or 9 of any suit.

Stayman Convention—The response of 2 Clubs to 1 Notrump asking opener to bid a four-card major suit.

stopper—High card that will stop the opponents from running a suit.

takeout double—A double that asks partner to bid his best suit.

trick—Four cards comprise one trick, one card being played by each player; there are 13 tricks in every hand of bridge.

trump—The suit named in the final bid, other than notrump; to ruff.

void—A holding of no cards in a suit.

vulnerable—A side that has won a game in a rubber.

DEVYN PRESS PUBLICATIONS
BRIDGE BOOKS

BARON-STEWART:
The Bridge Student Text —
   Vol. 1, for Beginning Players 4.95
   Vol. 2, for Intermediate Players 4.95
   Vol. 3, for Advanced Players 4.95
   Vol. 4, Defensive Play 4.95
The Bridge Teachers' Manual —
   Vol. 1, for Beginning Players 11.95
   Vol. 2, for Intermediate Players 11.95
   Vol. 3, for Advanced Players 11.95
   Vol. 4, Defensive Play 11.95
BARON-WOOLSEY:
Clobber Their Artificial Club 2.95
BERNSTEIN-BARON:
Do You Know Your Partner?................1.95
BLACKWOOD:
Complete Book of Opening Leads 12.95
BLACKWOOD-HANSON:
Card Play Fundamentals 5.95
EBER-FREEMAN:
Have I Got a Story for You...............7.95
FLANNERY:
The Flannery 2◇ Convention 7.95
GOODWIN:
Table Talk 5.95
Let's Play Cards: Great Card Games
   for Children 9.95
GORSKI:
Art of Logical Bidding 4.95
HARRIS:
Bridge Director's Companion 12.95
HARRISON:
Player's Guide to the Rules of Duplicate Bridge .9.95
JOHNSON:
Classic Bridge Quotes 6.95
KEARSE:
Bridge Conventions Complete 17.95
KELSEY:
Countdown to Better Bridge 9.95
101 Bridge Maxims 7.95
LAWRENCE:
How to Play Card Combinations 9.95
Dynamic Defense.........................9.95
Falsecards 9.95
How to Read the Opponents' Cards 7.95
Partnership Understandings 2.95
Play Bridge with Mike Lawrence 9.95
LAWRENCE-HANSON:
Winning Bridge Intangibles 2.95
PENICK:
Beginning Bridge Complete 6.95
Beginning Bridge Quizzes................6.95
POWELL:
Tickets to the Devil 5.95
REESE:
Play These Hands With Me................7.95
REESE-HOFFMAN:
Play It Again, Sam 7.95

ROSENKRANZ:
The Bidder's Game 12.95
Everything You Ever Wanted to
   Know About Trump Leads 7.95
Tips for Tops...........................9.95
ROSENKRANZ-TRUSCOTT:
Modern Ideas in Bidding 9.95
RUBENS-LUKACS:
Test Your Play as Declarer, Vol. 1, ...5.95
SHEINWOLD:
Bridge Puzzles, Vol. 1 ....5.95
Bridge Puzzles, Vol. 2 ....4.95
Bridge Puzzles, Vol. 3 ....4.95
STEWART-BARON:
The Bridge Book
   Vol. 1, for Beginning Players 7.95
   Vol. 2, for Intermediate Players 7.95
   Vol. 3, for Advanced Players 7.95
   Vol. 4, Defensive Play 7.95
WOLFF:
Bidding Challenge 6.95
WOOLSEY:
Matchpoints 9.95
Partnership Defense.....................8.95

BRIDGE COMPUTER PROGRAMS

Mike Lawrence's Bridge Dealer
   (IBM or Macintosh) 50.00
Tournament Bridge (IBM or Apple) 49.95

BRIDGE FLASHCARDS

TRUSCOTT-GORDY:
Standard Plays of Card Combinations.........6.95

BRIDGE PAMPHLETS

Championship Bridge Series —
   Volume 1 (#1-12) 9.95
   Volume 2 (#13-24) 9.95
   Volume 3 (#25-36) 9.95
   Future Champions' Bridge Series —
   Volume 1 (#1-12) 9.95
Hanson: Fingertip Bridge .... .95
Keenan: Roman Key Card Blackwood ..... .95
Stewart-Baron: How To Be A Good Partner .... .95

SPORTS TITLES

BARON-VON BORRIES:
Official Ky. Derby Quiz Book 11.95
BARON-RICE:
Official U. of Ky. Basketball Book 9.95
HILL-BARON:
The Amazing Basketball Book 8.95

**BUY DEVYN PRESS PRODUCTS AT YOUR FAVORITE BOOKSTORE,
SEND TO: DEVYN PRESS, 151 THIERMAN LN., LOUISVILLE, KY 40207
OR
CALL DEVYN PRESS TOLL FREE (1-800-626-1598)
TO ORDER ANY OF THE ABOVE ITEMS OR TO SEND FOR OUR
FREE CATALOG.**